Diary of a Facelift

Diary
of a
Facelift

TOYAH
WILLCOX

MICHAEL O'MARA BOOKS LIMITED

First published in Great Britain in 2005 by
Michael O'Mara Books Limited
9 Lion Yard, Tremadoc Road
London SW4 7NQ

A CIP catalogue record for this book
is available from the British Library

ISBN 1-84317-135-X

1 3 5 7 9 10 8 6 4 2

www.mombooks.com

Designed and typeset by Martin Bristow

Printed and bound in the UK by Bath Press

Photograph Acknowledgements
Page 1: © John Rogers/Rex Features (*above*), RetnaUK (*below*);
Page 2: © Rex Features (*above*), Sten Roseland/Rex Features (*below*);
Page 3: © Allstar/Cinetext (*below*); Page 4: © Chris Wood/
expresspictures.com (*above*), Jim Selby/Rex Features (*below*);
Page 5: © Tony Larkin/Rex Features; Page 6: © Alpha Press (*above*
and *middle*), Granada/Rex Features (*below*); Page 7: © Cameron
Laird/Rex Features; Page 8: © Anglia Television (*above left*);
Pages 9–11: © Toyah Willcox/Robert Fripp;
Pages 12–16: © Dean Stockings.

Disclaimer
The publisher and author disclaim any liability for accidents or
injuries that may occur as a result of acting upon any information
given in this book. Readers are advised to seek independent medical
advice from an appropriately qualified and experienced medical
practitioner before proceeding with cosmetic surgery of any kind.
Every effort has been made to ensure that the information in this
book is correct at the time of going to press.

CONTENTS

ACKNOWLEDGEMENTS

This book is dedicated to my husband Robert Fripp, who has never once in our nineteen-year relationship criticized my appearance, and who throughout my recovery supported me and gave me confidence.

I also dedicate this work to Dr Olivier Henry de Frahan, who is clearly a dedicated genius responsible for helping many women, children and men rediscover their self-esteem. Lastly I would like to thank Linda Meredith and Dr Patrick Bowler for their unfailing support, wisdom and advice.

FOREWORD

THIS BOOK IS A DIARY. It is not an advertisement and I have not received payment or any kind of discount for the surgery I have undergone. Everything documented in this diary is based on fact. I alone made the decision to have the surgical procedures that I finally chose to undergo, and I personally paid all the resulting bills associated with the treatment. Even though I have absolutely no regret about any of my experiences, and the results are exactly what I hoped for, I must emphasize to anyone who is considering any form of plastic surgery that it is vital for the individual to conduct detailed research into the various options available, and to take full responsibility for any choices that are eventually made.

The reason for this very public outing about my surgery is in response to the overwhelming number of nervous and anxious phone calls I have received in the last year from friends of friends in show business, who have been desperate to talk to someone with first-hand experience of this kind of major surgical procedure. It is a serious and nerve-racking journey and under no circumstances can it be entered into lightly. Before any decisions are taken, there are many things to take into consideration – the state of one's health is crucial in particular, but it is also important to be certain about what exactly it is that you want to change, to know what sort of treatment will be best for you, and to be confident enough not to settle for any old procedure.

Before my facelift I was in the same emotional state as these aforementioned acquaintances, uncertain of what steps to take, and concerned about the consequences of any future surgery. It is unfortunate that, owing to strict privacy laws and the unwillingness of many people to 'admit' to having had work done, medical experts are unable to send potential clients to see the results of those who have had surgical enhancements, which, if they could, would doubtless be of immense help to individuals who are still deliberating over whether to take a leap into the unknown. Though I respect this situation, I am also a very honest person, and I'm immensely proud of what my surgeon has achieved for me, so I have had no problem whatsoever in telling people about it and sharing my experiences.

All the people I refer to in this book are real and their stories are all true. In fact only one person requested that her name be changed because she has a public life and does not wish to reveal the fact that she has had any form of cosmetic enhancement, and so her pseudonym is indicated by an asterisk; similarly, two friends who were more than happy to talk about their experiences privately requested complete anonymity in this book, which I fully respect and understand, so I have omitted their names altogether. Everyone else I have mentioned was more than happy to be identified and included in this book.

This book is a diary of events relating to my personal experience. It describes my fears, my paranoia, my misunderstandings, my reasons for opting for surgery in the first place, and my joy at the outcome. I have decided not to hold back when describing my most anxious moments, because I believe it is important for every potential patient to be aware that anxiety is a natural part of the surgical process, and is not something that should be suppressed.

The reason for writing this book is simple: I feel passionately that there are too many people in this world who are entering into surgery in the wrong frame of mind as a result of being misinformed, unprepared and afraid. I hope the details of my experience will go some way to answering some of the questions that I believe only a former patient can respond to adequately and honestly. I also hope my story will offer protection and wise counsel to encourage those people considering surgery to research, research, research, and make considered and responsible choices. I would like to feel that by relating my own experiences, I might help dispel certain fears about this taboo subject, because although we are all unique, we are undoubtedly united in our fear of the unknown.

For me, as I believe it is for many others, this journey isn't about discovering eternal youth; it is about making our longevity, our ever-increasing lifespan more bearable through seeking a better quality of life.

PROLOGUE

WHAT I AM ABOUT TO UNDERGO is the last taboo. Ninety per cent of all women are unhappy with some part of their bodies, but the one area that is most vulnerable to our insecurities is the one part that holds the key to our souls, our personality. It expresses our emotions and the feelings in our heart; it is the one part that really identifies us as individuals. You neither want to be defined by your face nor judged by it, but you are and people do.

The face has more muscles than any other part of the body. It is where most of our senses conduct their work, through which we communicate our consciousness and awareness of the world around us. It is the first thing to be seen when we are born and invariably the last thing to be scrutinized as we die.

* * *

It is a blisteringly cold February morning in Paris; the kind of morning that should be spent lying in bed wrapped up in the arms of a loved one while gazing out of the window at the branches of the leafless trees swaying in a wintry breeze. Instead I am lying on an operating table, drowsy from a pre-op sedative, thinking of my parents and crying, wondering if they will ever forgive me if anything goes wrong. The problem is that I haven't told them I am here. Although they know I'm in Paris, they don't know *why* I am here. I've let them think that I was coming here on holiday, which pleased them greatly, as to them my happiness is paramount, and so they were overjoyed at the prospect of my spending a week alone with Robert, my husband, in this most romantic of European cities. The thought of deceiving them is making me cry even more. If they knew that I had finalized my will before leaving England they would be crawling up the wall with despair right now, wondering what on earth I had been planning. I told them that I wouldn't be able to phone for a few days, but that my husband would be in touch. So innocent were they of my true intentions that it didn't even occur to them to ask why I wouldn't be available to make my daily phone call.

If they could see what I see, their hearts would be beating just as hard as mine. For as long as I can remember I have always had a phobia of hospitals, mainly because I was taken to them constantly during childhood. I was born with skeletal problems, a twisted spine, twisted feet, a twisted lispy tongue – it was a twisted sort of childhood, really – which made regular hospital appointments inevitable, and caused my fears to grow with each visit. With all that in mind it suddenly struck me how crazy it was to find myself voluntarily in a place where I had sworn I would never go again.

The walls around me are so white they appear to shine like crystals. Machines everywhere are bleeping and droning. I haven't a clue what they do, and because of the language barrier that exists between me and the people who keep drifting in and out of this crisp futuristic operating room, I don't feel able to ask anyone. I realize that it is impossible for silence to exist within this strange environment; here everything hums, even the human voices on the other side of the door. I cannot see who is talking, and this dreamlike state I'm in is heightened by the effects of the sedative.

It's 8 a.m. in Britain and my father will be putting the kettle on. Hundreds of miles away in the heart of Paris, I'm here in a private clinic lying on a very hard operating table in a brightly lit operating theatre, surrounded by friendly faces in green overalls looking over me and smiling. I am cold and there is a drip in my right arm and an anaesthesia needle waiting for the white fluid to flow

into my left arm. I'm crying and I'm frightened and I
want my husband by my side. The nurse has noticed that
I am trembling with cold – or more accurately with the
fear that is gripping me – so she squeezes my arm and
puts a heated blanket over me. All the people here are
trying their best to talk English, and I'm pathetically
trying to converse in French while laughing at every
opportunity in case they wheel me back to my room
because they think I look too frightened to proceed to the
final stage. I've been waiting for this moment for twenty
years – nothing as trivial as fear is going to stop me now.

I don't care that I am semi-naked in a thin, green gown
that covers little and reveals too much. I don't care that I
am half-dressed among strangers, and nor do I care that
I am frightened, so terrified that I can smell the fear
oozing from my armpits, a natural human scent that
must surely accompany so many patients on their way
into life-changing operations.

This is my moment, my extremely personal moment. I
am about to give my life and my face and therefore my
career into the hands of a man I have met only three
times before. All I know about this man, my surgeon, is
that he is honourable and completely dedicated to his
work. He has pieced together children who have been
victims of accidents, and he has reinvented the faces of
cinema royalty and models with his natural touch. Surely
that is enough? When he enters the room I feel a sense of
relief; at least I have already formed a rapport with him.
As for everyone else in this room who surrounds me in
my partially dressed state, it feels like this is our first date
and I'm lying here like a strumpet in my saucy gown.

Dr Olivier Henry de Frahan couldn't be a better suitor
for my tired old face. When I look at him, tall, dark and
as focused as a bird of prey, I see a man who at some
time in his life could have chosen to be either an
international playboy or a creator of beauty. As I lie
waiting, I thank God he chose the latter. It strikes me

that he has the sort of panache and style that an Englishman could only buy on Savile Row.

This moment is more personal than any sexual act, and if I'd been able to have been conscious enough forty-six years ago, I'd have to say that this particular point in my life is surely more intimate than actually being born.

In three minutes' time a stranger will pump me full of white anaesthesia fluid and then another will cut me open. How trusting is that? I can assure you that this situation takes extraordinary faith.

I am not getting my breasts enlarged as a present from my husband, for all the world to look at and admire as a fashion accessory, and nor am I having liposuction so that I can show off my new waistline and wear tighter clothes. I am having a facelift, the one act, it seems, that no one is willing to talk about or admit to having had done, simply because they could be exposed to ridicule because of the attitudes of the ignorant. Where I am going thousands have been before, though most will not admit it. Many have gone on record saying they would never dream of such an action, including people I really admire. For example, supermodel Jerry Hall has stated that she wouldn't entertain the thought of plastic surgery, as do many of the Hollywood A-list. Unfortunately the vast majority of the women in the world are not happy with their lot. At the other end of the spectrum there are equally notable and brilliant women who have 'gone public' about their cosmetic enhancements, from Sharon Osbourne to Debbie Harry. The one common factor that puts all of us under the same critical spotlight is that the face is the one feature of the body that remains naked to the world.

Girls are actively encouraged to announce their boob enhancements, particularly as this kind of surgery is embraced by the media – it sells a small forest of magazines and papers daily – and is generally appreciated by the boys. But what about surgery that caters for the older woman? It seems that being frank about a facelift is a no-no – facelifts just aren't sexy.

* * *

In 1978 I was twenty years old with skin as smooth and luminous as a white pearl. Strangers, women in particular, would compliment me on the beauty of my skin, and photographers positively cooed about the appearance of this miraculous formation of cells that covered my face. It's unfortunate, but true to say, that when you're twenty it's *only* skin to you; in your youth, it doesn't really occur to you that one day that 'skin' of yours is going to turn to parchment while you're still inhabiting it . . .

In this same year I made a film with the legendary actress Katharine Hepburn. *The Corn Is Green* was an American remake of the Emlyn Williams classic about an ambitious schoolmistress from the Smoke, who travels to a mining town in Wales to educate exploited miners. After auditioning alongside more than 2,000 hopefuls, I was cast as the strumpet who gets pregnant by the school prodigy. Presented with the opportunity to be directed by film legend George Cukor – the man who immortalized Marilyn Monroe – and to act alongside Katharine Hepburn, I embarked not only on a movie of a lifetime, but also on a relationship beyond all others.

Katharine Hepburn was like no other woman I had ever known. To begin with she was an icon – a status she certainly hadn't attained through luck. In my eyes her talent was awe-inspiring. She was extraordinarily handsome with a carved, defined beauty, and with a stature that comes from sustained pride – a pride that would have been necessary when spending most of her life in the stifling environment of a youth-obsessed Hollywood. It was obvious that she had had to fight from all corners at some point in her life.

When I acted with her I found myself looking into eyes that were crystal clear; her skin was porcelain smooth, and her figure trim and straight, still boyish in fact. She was in her early seventies when we worked together, and boy, was she luminescent! She exuded vitality, and remained a truly fantastic actress despite her battle with Parkinson's disease; indeed, as soon as the cameras began rolling she would always succeed in keeping a posture of complete stillness.

Despite being blessed with as great and unrivalled a talent as hers, I would learn that Katharine Hepburn hadn't been able to avoid adversity or negativity on the road to success, having experienced the most appalling abuse about her looks from the moment her career began until it neared its end. Once, during a lunch with her and George Cukor, Katharine told me how the critics had analysed her first performance on stage in Washington, DC. They described how her cheekbones were too high, her hair was a tangled mess, that she looked like a man, her voice was a cackle and her movements were wooden. Naturally her family were in the audience to see her first night, and the next day were as devastated by the reviews as she was; her mother was reported to be beside herself from the shame of it all.

Katharine Hepburn's first stage critiques were not about her work, but merely about how she looked. Even while sitting with her in 1978 I could feel the hurt that this memory evoked in her. This gracious, generous and outstandingly beautiful human being seemed to have spent her entire Hollywood career carrying the burden of these insults, which were no doubt long forgotten by those who wrote them. To me, when I looked into her face I saw a beauty that was completely natural – a wise beauty.

Back then, however, I was too young, too unaware of the effects of time, to appreciate fully what Katharine had been through. One reason she never succumbed to the surgeon's knife was because she was too strong in her self-opinion. I wouldn't say that she was strong in her confidence, because I saw immense vulnerability in her, but her strong sense of self meant that she could never surrender to peer pressure, no matter how intensely it was imposed.

It's my belief that because of her own difficult history in the movie business she was unusually protective towards me, always taking time to nurture and compliment me as a person and as an actress. I never knew quite what I meant to her, though she repeatedly said we were alike in personality and she wished she could have been a punk rocker, which I still remained underneath the period wig and the corseted costume I wore in the film. I had bright red hair that she called 'the feathers', and she would touch it at every possible opportunity, often asking the director, 'George! Do you think this would suit me?'

At the time I felt that the interest she showed me stemmed simply from her natural generosity of spirit, but five years later, when I had achieved fame of my own, I was sent a copy of her autobiography, *Me: Stories of My Life*, and was surprised to discover that she had written a few sentences about me. In a chapter devoted to *The Corn Is Green*, she described her impressions of me during the casting: 'A girl walked in by the name of Toyah Willcox. Five feet tall. Tiny waist. Big bosom. Skin like the inside of a shell. Eyes . . . full of thoughts. Wicked thoughts. Suggesting so much. And so much fun too. Loves life . . .'

Though I think that Katharine probably sensed there was something unusual about me (apart from my bright red punky hair), what she didn't know about me was that I was used to imperfection. I was born with a twisted spine, clawed feet, a clubbed (unusually large) right foot and one leg that's two inches longer than the other. Also, the roof of my mouth is too high, which duly caused the speech impediment that others call a lisp. When I was a child, surgeons offered to amputate my right leg below the knee. My mother refused. I needed to be taught how to walk and talk until the age of eleven. My mother carried out most of this education, forever terrified that the world would perceive me as disabled. In fact it was my mother who taught me to project the illusion of normality.

So I know a great deal about imperfection and I know even more about hiding it. What is extraordinary to me is that no matter how well you appear to disguise your disabilities, other people seem to have an unconscious in-built awareness that you are not one of them, i.e. 'one of the perfect ones'. In most cases they respond to you differently without even being aware of what they are doing. If we were all animals in the jungle I would have been attacked long ago for my weakness, but in the civilized world that kind of physical reaction has been replaced by verbal and written criticism.

What upsets me about Katharine Hepburn's experiences is that she was a natural and unusual beauty. She didn't fit into any of the moulds that other women did at that time in history, therefore she was perceived negatively, and criticized by others for being unusual and, to them, freakishly ugly. In newspapers especially, the power of the written word is tangible, and in her case the early reviews of her work were unjust and caused her deep emotional scarring.

It was while working on this film that I met a make-up artist whom Miss Hepburn had transported from America to be at her side. Like most make-up people he could render a room silent with a fantastically indiscreet yarn. I cannot remember his name or all of his tales, but I can remember one story that he related.

In the 1950s, when film stars really were creatures of the firmament and worshipped like gods and goddesses, the ageing process was a bitter and cruel blow to those who, throughout their youth, had enjoyed blessed and beautiful lives. It was mostly the actresses who suffered, the only two 'options' available to these women being either to surrender to the ravages of age or to suffer a tragic death. In the meantime, however, these stars began to go to extraordinary lengths to prolong their mystery and extend their working lives. The make-up artist told me that in these earlier days, egg white was used as a serum to prolong the image of youth. Possibly used by Cleopatra 6,000 years ago, the substance had been rediscovered by desperate make-up artists who had the arduous responsibility for maintaining a star's beauty in the golden age of Hollywood. The egg white would be painted on to the actress's face, before the application of any make-up, and as long as the star didn't express herself too excessively, it would hold her face smooth for many takes before eventually cracking. It is interesting to consider how many times we have heard critics glory the composure of certain film luminaries, when it was most likely the fear of the egg white flaking off that kept these individuals so poised.

But by far the oddest, saddest and most desperate attempt at delaying the passing of one's youth was rumoured to have been carried out by one of the most famous actresses of all time. This story has reached the status of urban legend in the world of film, but I first heard it from a make-up artist on the film *Quadrophenia*, in which I played a leading character alongside Sting, Leslie Ash and Phil Daniels. I have heard it a few times since on different film shoots, though attached to different actresses, so I can't help feeling that it's probably true and that many women in the movie world used this technique.

When I heard this story for the first time it was attached to an actress in her fifties who had won an Oscar for a role in which she played a faded starlet. She had been one of the leading beauties in her younger days, but while her looks were beginning to fade, her ambition grew stronger. Such was her desire to remain a key Hollywood player, she allowed her personal make-up artist to use a hair grip to pierce the skin at the sides of her head in her hairline. Once the grip had penetrated the skin behind her ear, he would then twist and turn the skin round until her face tightened up, before securing the pin under her wig.

At the time I wasn't convinced about the truth behind this story, so I phoned a friend whom I trusted would confirm its credibility. He was an actor called Tim, whose father had been a stuntman on all the major Hollywood films of the 1950s and 1960s, and by association had had the privilege of being acquainted with a lot of the major stars. As Tim was a child at the time of his father's involvement in various films, he had been allowed entry into behind-the-scenes areas, where he doubtless heard many a Hollywood tale, and thus he was able to verify that the story I had heard was indeed true.

'Not only that, but Marlene Dietrich wore a gossamer-thin gold chain made specially by a jeweller that ran across the top of her head and under her chin,' he revealed. 'The chain could be tightened at the top of her head, which in turn pulled her neck tight, and then a wig was placed on top.'

I replied that it seemed a terribly sad thing to have to do to maintain her star status, and he added, 'Well, it wasn't only her face, her body had no curves. She was as straight as a stick, so all her costumes were upholstered and padded to give the illusion of a fuller figure. Once, during a show, she fell off stage into the orchestra pit, and she refused to be moved until all the audience had left the theatre. It wasn't that she was hurt – the padding in her dress had dislodged and she didn't want anyone to see it. Apparently her dresses were so reupholstered they stood up on their own!'

This was something of a revelation to me, the fact that what everyone assumed to have been Dietrich's naturally curvaceous figure had actually been artificially created. Of course she wasn't the only movie star to go to great lengths to enhance their looks. Many Hollywood starlets had nose jobs in the name of vanity and career survival before they became established in the movie world. It was almost like adopting a uniform; their noses all looked the same, as if they had been bought off the peg.

However, it is also important to remember that aside from the cosmetic desire for corrective procedures among certain actors and actresses, there have also been cases of non-commercial plastic surgery in tinsel town, for example when reconstructive surgery has been necessary following a devastating accident. Ava Gardner was once kicked in the face by a horse while filming in Spain and needed extensive plastic surgery to save not only her life but also her career. Who would ever have guessed, as she has always looked like a true natural beauty. While filming *Raintree County* in 1957 with Elizabeth Taylor, Hollywood heart-throb Montgomery Clift suffered almost fatal injuries when, after having dinner with his co-star at her home one evening, the car he was driving hit a telegraph pole. Elizabeth Taylor ran to the scene of the accident and saved his life by putting her fingers down his throat to clear the broken teeth from his windpipe. Filming had to stop for weeks while surgeons wired his jaw and patched up his face. Even after all this trauma he returned to the set physically and mentally scarred, and could only be shot from one particular angle because nerve damage had paralysed part of his face. When I hear stories such as these I gain a new respect for the work of reconstructive surgeons because all too often they are associated solely with the beauty industry and accused of pandering to people's vanity.

Cosmetic surgery certainly isn't new. Contrary to popular belief it isn't even an invention of the last hundred years, a century where film, TV and magazine publishing have set new aesthetic standards. According to the American Society of Plastic Surgeons there exists visual evidence that proves that forms of plastic surgery were practised on facial injuries among the ancient Egyptians as far back as 4000 BC. It's hard to envisage how such procedures were handled so long ago – did three slaves sit on the patient and a physician work as fast as he could, attaching cow skin to the wound? One can only imagine and presume that the methods were as prehistoric as fossilized dinosaur bones, but as time wore on, progress was indeed being made. In fact there is evidence of incredibly intricate surgical procedures being carried out around 800 BC, which not only sounds miraculous, but also makes one wonder how it was possible that mankind could be so medically advanced before the concept of the common germ was understood.

In India, 800 years before the birth of Christ, surgeons found themselves in great demand, deriving considerable profit from the tragedies that befell others, particularly those who had been brutally punished for leading a life of crime. Operations not so far removed from plastic-surgery procedures in use today were being carried out in the poorest villages and fields of India by travelling surgeons. The most common surgery was performed upon thieves and pickpockets. In the country at this time it was the custom to cut off the noses of people found guilty of robbery and adultery, which left such individuals forever associated with wrongdoing of some kind, unable to escape from their past mistakes and doomed to remain outcasts for life.

The only escape from this life-sentence of dishonour was to go through the agony of having a new nose reconstructed. Surgeons would take a vine leaf and after tracing around the nose area they would then flip the leaf upwards and remove that exact area of skin from the forehead, peel it down, rotate it and then rebuild the criminal's nose. The bravery it must have taken to endure such an operation, simply to help disguise the stigma of petty crime or unfaithfulness, was extraordinary, yet the idea of undergoing it without anaesthesia is almost unthinkable. Today, such a procedure is called 'forehead rhinoplasty' or 'forehead nasal construction'; in those days it was called desperation.

Progress in plastic surgery didn't start to accelerate until the nineteenth and twentieth centuries thanks to the strengthening scientific and medical establishments in Europe and America. One of America's early pioneers in plastic surgery was the highly eminent Dr John Peter Mettauer. A brilliant gynaecologist as well as a progressive surgeon, in 1827 he successfully corrected a cleft palate using instruments that he had designed himself, and throughout his career he performed numerous operations that had never before been attempted in the US.

In Europe, progress was being made in aesthetic plastic surgery in the late 1800s thanks to the ground-breaking work of a Prussian surgeon, Dr Jacques Joseph. Widely regarded as the pioneer of rhinoplasty, he presented his endo-nasal techniques to the Medical Society of Berlin in 1898, and later he began carrying out corrective surgery on the human nose, the precursor to today's endo-nasal rhinoplasty. For Jewish people who had faced discrimination with regard to their physical characteristics, Joseph's work offered them an escape from the prejudices of nineteenth-century society. Of Jewish descent himself, Jacques Joseph noted that although cosmetic surgery was not a physical necessity, it was worthwhile because of its positive effect on a person's spirit and personality. Regarding the human spirit, however, it wasn't until after the Second World War that the medical world began to accept that certain types of 'cosmetic' surgery – nicknamed 'psychiatry with a scalpel' – were legitimate ways of curing emotional or personal problems.

Developments in plastic surgery quickened with the onset of war in the early twentieth century. Though the steel helmet had been introduced to the trenches in 1915, this still left the face vulnerable and many casualties of war were terrifyingly disfigured. The nature of the horrific wounds being inflicted on thousands of soldiers during the First World War meant that rapid advances in surgical procedures were needed desperately. Shocking facial injuries such as shattered jaws, missing noses and badly-burned skin were increasingly being suffered by many of the soldiers returning from the front line, which meant that innovative and effective new treatments were essential.

While serving as a field doctor with the Royal Army Medical Corps, Harold Gillies quickly recognized the need to give specialist treatment to soldiers with serious facial wounds, and having consulted other surgeons and medical journals before the war, he was able to learn how to repair jaw injuries using bone and tissue from other parts of the body. After the Battle of the Somme in 1916 he found himself responsible for 2,000 patients, some of whom needed their entire faces rebuilding. It was at this time that he created the procedure known as the 'tubed pedicle graft', an innovation that made it possible to transfer skin from one part of the body to another while maintaining the blood supply. Gradually, Dr Gillies grew adept at making skin flaps to reconstruct mouths, noses and ears in an attempt to conceal many different disfigurements, so that when these war victims went back into society they would not be shunned or encounter hostility. It is because of his work that we have some of the instruments and techniques commonly used today.

But for every score of good surgeons there was at least one quack. An American, Dr John Howard Crum, not only advertised in the Yellow Pages, which would have been unheard of in the medical profession, he also carried out facelifts in front of invited audiences. In 1931 he performed the first-recorded public facelift on an actress in the Grand Ballroom of the Pennsylvania Hotel in New York, and later did several others, reportedly accompanied by a pianist playing popular tunes.

Using only novocaine (a substance normally used by dentists to numb patients' gums), which he injected all over the woman's face, he performed a successful but scandalous operation, later commenting, 'It's just like peeling a banana!' Perhaps he was hoping it would grow in popularity in the way that 'lunch-hour' Botox has today.

* * *

In the last hundred years fashions have changed so much. In the 1920s women wanted flat chests; in the 1950s the waist was small and the bust high; and in 2004 the bust is almost comical in its supposedly 'ideal' representation, with young women commonly demanding melon-sized implants.

Cosmetic surgery is no longer exclusively set aside for those fighting against the ageing process or for individuals who consider they have abnormalities. It is an option that is available to everyone who can afford it if they feel they need to boost their confidence or pep up their sexuality with a little nip and tuck.

It is refreshing, therefore, to discover stories of people who resist the obvious. Fanny Brice, the Broadway star upon whom the film and stage play *Funny Girl* is based, was a Jewess. She decided to have her nose straightened, which caused much comment in the society press of America. Famously, the wickedly witty Dorothy Parker declared that 'Fanny cut off her nose to spite her race.' But the story does not end there. When Barbra Streisand appeared on Broadway in the title role of *Funny Girl* some forty years later, there was major speculation as to why she hadn't had her own nose straightened before embarking on a career in show business. Miss Streisand ignored the pressure and went on to achieve world acclaim from an audience who loved her just the way she was.

For almost twenty years I have been contemplating cosmetic surgery. I was probably in my late twenties when, in front of the bathroom mirror, I started a daily ritual of dragging my skin tight with my fingers and wondering how I would improve with a bit of a nip and a tuck. I wasn't bothered about my breasts or other parts of my body, which could be disguised with good clothes, high-quality tailoring and flattering colours – it was just my face that was causing me concern. My skin, which had previously been so luminous, was ageing rapidly. From my early twenties I was subject to constant pressure to change parts of my face that were hard to light on film, particularly under my eyes, which had started to look tired and dark-shadowed.

My emotions, it seems, were never secret; they etched themselves across my face, embarrassing me, revealing my insecurities, leaving nothing to the imagination. Insecurities about everything from work to family carved deep unattractive lines above my brows and hormonal changes thinned my lips, giving the overall appearance not of someone who belongs to the carefree glamorous world of show business, but of a person who had spent too much of her life worrying instead of partying. In showbiz land no one is free to display the private and personal side of their lives; it's only really possible to air your emotions if there's an Oscar in one hand and an acceptance speech in the other. But it's when your guard is down that true feelings are inevitably captured in the split-second snap of a paparazzo's camera shutter.

In 1983 I was twenty-five and had been cast with Sir Laurence Olivier in a high-profile TV film called *The Ebony Tower*. Because we were working with such a major star, the film was taken as seriously as if we had been shooting a Hollywood blockbuster. We had the best cameramen, the best lighting crew and the best director available. It was during a break in filming one day that one of the men responsible for lighting took me aside and told me that he was finding it impossible to light my eyes and disguise the lines I had beneath them. He was completely honest with me and said that there was only so much he could do professionally, before suggesting that I should give serious thought to having some surgery, to sort out the problems that my tired old eyes were causing.

Though he may have sounded brutal, he was right and was telling me something that many acquaintances – from managers to hairdressers – had hinted at before. I hadn't a clue about what I should do or where I should go, as up until that point I hadn't had much faith in cosmetic surgery, and consequently hadn't given it a thought. Also part of me felt I was too young for this kind of operation. I was still in my twenties after all, and was convinced that this sort of surgery was reserved for the older woman, at least those aged forty and upwards. I liked my face and was happy with the way I looked. Indeed, I was proud of my looks, and even though I had had the usual taunts in the press about weight (despite weighing just over 7 stone), I knew I was looking after myself and keeping fit. Nonetheless the seeds of doubt were being sown and while I grew older, I became increasingly aware of the waves of younger stars who kept arriving on the scene.

Psychologically I felt that sustaining a successful career was going to get more and more difficult unless I acted upon the advice that I'd received from various quarters, but at this time in my life I was convinced there were no trustworthy surgeons in England. Everyone was telling me to go to LA or Switzerland, but I had neither sufficient financial back-up nor enough time to conduct any thorough research, and in any case the world of plastic surgery was notoriously hard to research in the early 1980s. Part of me remained adamant that I was far too young to walk down that path just yet, and so I decided to live with my lot and accept things as they were, while making sure that I kept to a good, healthy lifestyle. In retrospect I'm pleased I did because surgery carried out twenty years ago actually *looks* like surgery; none of it looks natural. Each surgeon seems to have stamped their style on the faces of their clients like a calling card. In general I liked my face as it was, and just wanted to get rid of the permanently tired look, which I was concerned would give the negative impression that I was forever stressed by the commitments associated with my fame.

By the time I was twenty-nine I had become seriously concerned about how much I was beginning to age, especially as six years earlier I'd noticed that the skin beneath my eyes had started to stretch. It was evident that I hadn't inherited those genes that keep some lucky people young-looking, well into their sixties. So in 1987 I decided to do as much research as possible to discover where most people seemed to be going for 'corrective procedures'. I kept arriving at dead ends or being advised only to 'have surgery in Switzerland', which wasn't much help back then. Adverts had started to appear in the back of magazines from *Vogue* to *Harper's Bazaar*, but because I didn't know anyone who had called the numbers and couldn't rely on recommendations, such details were useless to me. The only information my friends would impart was about whom to avoid in the medical profession, while relating terrible stories of drunken mutilations. They refused to tell me which practitioners were definitely worth consulting, keeping the names a jealously guarded secret. My gut instinct told me that wild horses couldn't extract the facts I needed from my friends. I could be looking them in the eyes knowing they had had surgery – good surgery, it was obvious – yet they would deny it and put me off with some horror story. It became blatantly clear that the world I was trying to enter was a closed shop, to me at least. I was trying to find a surgeon in a culture of impenetrable secrecy.

One of my closest friends at the time, a Kuwaiti princess who lived in Mayfair, had had facial surgery while at finishing school in Switzerland, which I only heard about from a passing comment that she made; no surgeon's name was offered. One evening she invited me to her apartment to meet Imelda Marcos – wife of the former Philippine dictator Ferdinand. It was a wildly exciting prospect, and I promised her I wouldn't mention shoes or stare at Imelda's feet.

When Imelda arrived she was accompanied by her two daughters. They were both elegant and attractive girls with restrained graceful manners, whom I imagined were in their early to mid teens. She was intending to present them to London society and this was to be one of their first evenings out on the social circuit, as it had been planned that various luminaries were going to pop over and say hello in the safe environment of my friend's home.

On being introduced to Imelda I approached her with a big friendly smile (something I would do automatically when meeting anyone for the first time), but in response I was rewarded with a surprising though gentle warning from Imelda: 'You mustn't smile, my dear. It will give you wrinkles.' My reaction was part amusement and part astonishment! However, she had obviously impressed on her own daughters the importance of this advice, for as I looked at the two beautiful girls it was clear that not a single smile passed their lips no matter how humorous the situation. In fact as events became less formal during the course of the evening, and the usual clowning around ensued, I saw that the girls literally had to try to stop themselves from laughing by holding their faces with their hands, to the extent that they were almost rocking backwards and forwards in discomfort.

So concerned was I that they were missing out on one of the greatest pleasures and therapies in life, that I had to ask them how long they were planning to avoid ever laughing or smiling. I certainly couldn't understand how they were ever going to flirt with boys otherwise. They responded to me as if I were verging on insanity: 'But if you keep using your face like this, creasing it with so many expressions, you will grow old before your time . . .'

They may have had a point, but to go through life having taken the conscious decision not to laugh no matter how funny a situation was not for me, so at the tender age of twenty-nine I began my quest to find a surgeon who could save me.

Eventually, through gossip, friends and the few magazine articles available on the subject in the 1980s, I found two names that consistently cropped up. The first was a man in his late fifties, who, rumour had it, was almost on the verge of retirement so I had to act quickly to schedule a meeting with him. Certain friends had told me that they knew people who had had work done by him and that he was one of the best surgeons available in England at that time. Although I hadn't seen any of his post-operative clients, I was still reassured by the recommendations. His office was on Harley Street, which I also assumed was a sign of his top professional status. When I took a seat in the waiting area, I noticed I was sharing the room with a number of fairly overweight female 'sixty-somethings', which was slightly off-putting, as I'd much rather have seen some young ambitious models waiting for a subtle 'tweak'.

During my consultation, to which he arrived late, he didn't seem the least bit interested. He studied my eyes for a few moments, then rather dismissively and bombastically said, 'Speak to my secretary, she'll book you in when I'm available in three months. It will cost £4,000. Thank you.' That was the sum of his consultation! I wasn't even invited to ask any questions despite having plenty on my mind; I particularly wanted to know exactly what he was going to do, to learn more about his procedures. What really put me off was the arrogance, the assumption that I was going to put my face in his hands unquestioningly. I could just imagine the scene, waking up after the operation wanting and needing reassurances but discovering that he's too important to answer questions. There was no way I could put my trust in such a person, even if he was one of the top surgeons in England.

The second doctor I visited was much younger and was rumoured to have carried out miraculous work on young up-and-coming supermodels of the moment, so my expectations were high. As I entered his office on Wimpole Street I was confronted by a man in his late twenties who really couldn't convince me that he'd amassed enough experience to have a solid 100 per cent success rate. I was too shy to ask what might be construed as an impertinent question about the level of his expertise.

He sat me down and carefully studied my face. Bearing in mind that I was there just to have my eyes improved, I was told, 'Yes, I will make an incision here [indicating from the top of my right ear, over the top of my head to the top of my left ear], then I will peel your face right down to the nose and restructure the muscles on your face.' My mind was made up on the spot – I definitely wouldn't be going to him!

Surely I was too young to have anything that drastic and serious done to my face? I couldn't help but think that it would have been the equivalent of voluntary mutilation but with a whacking great bill at the end of it. Having entered the clinic with the intention of only having my eyes done because I was perfectly happy with the rest of my face, I came out and decided to cease my quest for surgery there and then.

But was the surgeon right? Looking back, should I have started having cosmetic procedures earlier, despite my youth? Recently I have heard rumours that a certain well-known pop star started having 'facial adjustments' in her twenties, and now, in her mid-thirties, she looks sensational. At the time, I found it shocking that women in their twenties were being advised to have full facelifts, and I began to wonder whether money was the overriding factor in all of this madness, or whether there was indeed a growing demand among the young. Either way, after becoming confused about and mistrustful of people's true motives, I decided never to seek surgery in England.

When I reached my forties I heard a strong and persistent rumour in the world of show business claiming that it is advisable to have your first facelift in your forties because it will last longer. More than a decade after my original forays into the world of plastic surgery, techniques and anaesthetics had advanced so much that the recovery time was more manageable and the results more subtle. Though my thoughts had turned back to journeying down the surgical path once again at this time, I was not looking to relive my younger days, as I didn't feel that youth is all it's cracked up to be. On the contrary, I loved being in my forties, and was simply looking to fulfil ambitions and enjoy middle-age without my appearance being an issue in the battle against tired old ageist attitudes.

* * *

In September 2003 I was exhausted after a year of touring in the title role of *Calamity Jane*. The experience had been fantastic, but it had certainly taken its toll. I looked haggard and gaunt, and no amount of sleep could cure the tiredness etched on my face. This was the final straw. I felt so bad about my appearance that I couldn't look in the mirror without my heart sinking.

Professionally, I was starting to find myself in the situation of being highly qualified but working increasingly in a younger environment. That wasn't what was bothering me, however, as I really love being my age.

What was getting to me was the fact that my contemporaries seemed to be growing ever more youthful with every day that passed, and I didn't know how they were achieving it; nor would any of them share their age-defying secrets with me. Also it was becoming apparent to me that regardless of how hard you had worked in the past and in recent times, no matter how many accolades you had won, if your face and arse are no longer pretty then no one wants to look at you. As someone very much in the business of being looked at, I had to make sure that all my assets were in the best shape ever.

In the past if I put on weight I noticed a difference in the way that people regarded me. For instance in my thirties, which I affectionately call my 'hormonal heffalump years', I was two stone heavier. As a consequence it seemed I was being ignored by the opposite sex. I had lost the mandatory size eight tag and 'shazam' . . . I had become as invisible as a single working mother of ten who runs her world efficiently while not officially existing in the eyes of the male population, and I found that scary.

Now, in the present, I was starting to notice that people no longer looked me in the eyes, as if they had been unconsciously programmed to consider only aesthetically pleasing features. I admit that I found this quite devastating as I'd always assumed that people talked to me because of who I was and not for how I looked. It was a real wake-up call, especially as I have a lot of life left in me and there's a great deal more I would like to achieve. Once I'd become aware that this was happening to me, I learned an even bigger lesson when it dawned on me that I adopted exactly the same attitude with other people. Are we judgemental as a species? Are we born like this or has media saturation brainwashed us to appreciate only surface values?

So it was at this point in my life that once again I kick-started my quest to find a surgeon with whom I could take this giant 'leap', because a 'leap' is how it feels; a 'leap of faith' into unknown territory. Although modern facelift technology has been developing for almost a hundred years, and we all know there are surgeons and clinics out there, nobody can tell how good these professionals really are until we've actually experienced the process ourselves. It's all down to personal taste.

There is no excuse not to research today. The Internet has created the best opportunity to explore the procedures you want, giving people so much more access to information than ever before. When I typed in 'good plastic surgery' on my computer keyboard one day, the first thing that came up on my screen was an advert for the world's first plastic-surgery contest – 'Miss Artificial Beauty' – which was due to be held in China in December 2004. I couldn't quite see it catching on somehow, when the whole concept of the event relies heavily upon surgically enhanced goddesses revealing that their beauty really is skin deep . . . because it's completely fake. How many women would be willing to reveal something so private, I wondered.

The Internet is brilliant at introducing you to new surgical techniques and educating you in the 'lingo' of plastic-surgery land, which is vital to avoid being bamboozled into looking at a web page you never wanted to see in the first place. What the Web cannot tell you, however, are the success rates associated with the various types of surgery. Furthermore, websites don't reveal what the scars will look like, which I would have found reassuring. One site on *www.emedicine.com* was advertising 231 different procedures from 'lower extremity reconstruction' to 'repairing malpractice'. How do you choose? I can almost understand the practice of answering the breast-enlargements ads in the back of magazines, firstly because it's convenient and, at worst, if you come away with an unsightly scar you can at least cover those bazookas with clothes for most of the time, but with facelifts any scarring cannot be so easily concealed – the face bares the soul. Your face is the most exposed part of your body. The surgery and surgeon you choose have got to be the best you can find.

It's easy to think that when you look in the ads sections you are spoilt for choice, because not only can you get your face, boobs, tummy and thighs tucked, I also discovered one clinic that promises to give you an 'aesthetically pleasing vagina'; perhaps they teach it to say, 'Darling, your face is so beautiful!' I couldn't help but doubt whether anyone actually cared about 'aesthetically pleasing vaginas'. Can't these surgeons improve any of the pricks we all know instead (metaphorically speaking)?!

Breast enlargement is by far the most common and popular surgical procedure among women, which is why you can probably even find ads for it in the local parish magazines that come through your door. It's obvious why it's in such great demand when there are hordes of young women out there who feel increasingly inadequate about their breasts as a result of being confronted with the media's ever-increasing coverage of boob-job devotees. With pop stars and glamour models setting the standards higher and higher by insisting on being enlarged to 34 DD and beyond, the planet is going to run out of silicone, and it isn't a recyclable resource. In fact it won't be long until the graveyards of Los Angeles will start to groan under the weight of breast implants that will never rot. So bear that in mind if you ever go for a boob job – part of you will live on for ever.

Back to my generation and our well-developed jowls, there have been some notable success stories of people in the public eye who, far from wanting to keep their surgery a secr et, have taken the bold step of 'outing' themselves in the press after having facelifts. Big, beautiful stars have been quoted in the press admitting to their surgery, though I presume the motivation behind such honesty has been to counter unwanted press intrusion, and to ensure that any revealing insights are released to the public on their own terms. Little is said about those personalities whose surgery has been a success; the cases we hear about constantly are always those that are negatively reported, thereby discrediting the field of cosmetic surgery as a whole and unfairly casting all plastic surgeons in a bad light. Michael Jackson is a key figure who hits the headlines for all the wrong reasons; it seems that the whole world is waiting for his face to fall off. Even Cher – who looks bloody good for her wonderful age – gets too many cheeky headlines along the lines of 'How many facial expressions has Cher got?'

One of the major success stories in this quest for self-improvement is Sharon Osbourne. It has been alleged that she weighed 14 stone before she had her stomach stapled, and prior to her facelift photographs of her have revealed quite a plain and ordinary-looking person, but now she is one of the most beautiful women in the world, and has rightly chosen to go public about her surgery. Another example of success, Debbie Harry, has revealed that she has had a facelift, and at the age of fifty-nine she looks classy and confident. By far my favourite diva is Dolly Parton, who may look as though she has had more chest surgery than Jordan, but as she freely admits, 'When I look in the mirror and see something I don't like, I just pop along for a nip 'n' tuck.' Good on her for her honesty.

These are all women who have reinvented themselves, indeed who have felt compelled to reinvent themselves. It would be a brave choice if Debbie or Dolly had allowed themselves to grow to a size eighteen with faces representing the map of the Colorado mountains. I imagine that Sharon Osbourne probably realized she had more to offer the world than being condemned to live in her husband's shadow managing his career from the sidelines, and that if she was to be taken seriously in her own right a bit of serious styling was needed. With Ms Harry and Ms Parton the reason is patently obvious – the world would never let them grow old in peace. It would be waiting behind hidden cameras for the moment that little old lady popped out of them. Thankfully, they are still working, still being photographed and still in demand. It's almost as if they owe it to us to be beautiful. I adore these women for their candid honesty, and I neither want to ridicule nor persecute them. I am so grateful to them for being able to admit to the world that they have had a little help in sustaining their allure.

Mine is a different story. I am not a world-renowned beauty (what a burden that must be), and so mine is a situation that I think is all too common and it's the real reason why the cosmetic beauty industry is booming in the twenty-first century. My truth, which I freely admit, is that I have a body-dysmorphic problem. No matter how hard I work to look good, and to be fit and healthy, I cannot quite see the true me. There are too many layers, like sediment, from my emotional past that combine to distort my self-image. Some thin girls look in the mirror and see a fat person. Some overweight people look in the mirror and see a thin person. I look in the mirror and I see my mother's fears – her worries that I will not be a perfect representation of her, and her concerns that I will fail. I hear her criticism of me as a child and I see who my mother has become in her old age. The lines on her face will become the lines on mine and the weight on her hips I will inherit too. By writing this I am not pointing the finger of blame; I am simply observing that while most boys are brought up to believe they are perfect, girls are generally brought up to believe they are imperfect.

As a teenager I really didn't appreciate puberty. When my breasts first appeared at the age of eleven it was fun for a while, choosing 'trainer' bras and witnessing my T-shirts defy gravity, but the problem was I kept growing and growing. By the time I was twelve I was a 32D. It was freakish. I didn't even know the facts of life at this age, but still had to deal with being the focus of inappropriate attention and mind-boggling comments, the likes of, 'Oooh! Little girl, you've got big ones. Can I have a feel?' It's sad but true that men at bus stops in the 1970s would ask me anything from 'Which horse won the 2.30 at Lingfield?' to 'What do you wear under your school shirt?'

When I hit fourteen I rebelled at home and at school. The feelings of conformity were stifling. I had to dress like *this* (dresses and frills) and I had to act like *that* (sugar and spice and all things nice). I felt I was being raised to live a lie as nothing about me felt female. It wasn't a pleasure to play with dolls, it was an insult, and as for adhering to the laws imposed on my gender, I really didn't want anything to do with being feminine. I didn't have a problem with my sexual orientation, it was just that I felt an overwhelming need to be seen as a person and not to be judged and patronized on account of my being female. Once I left home at the age of eighteen I seriously wanted to create a gender-free 'movement', an androgynous organization of like-minded people who didn't want to live their lives imprisoned by gender clichés such as servile women who are treated like doormats, or predatory women who compulsively flirt, or women who hate other women. The way society was in the 1970s, it all felt so false and 'programmed'. Already at a young age I was insecure in my body.

I have found that these early insecurities have a way of staying with you no matter how many layers of 'life experience' time heaps upon them, as every now and then something comes along that causes them to surface again. For me it happened at the end of 2003, after I had completed the gruelling West End run in *Calamity Jane*. It was a physically demanding show and our run took place during some of the hottest days on record. Consequently I was feeling like a wounded prune when I should have been celebrating a fantastic achievement.

Prior to appearing in the stage show, I had been living in the Australian jungle, while taking part in the second series of the reality-TV show *I'm A Celebrity, Get Me Out Of Here!* The arduous twelve days spent in the wild was certainly worth it as I'd managed to raise £70,000 for my chosen charity, which was another achievement that should have made me proud, but sadly the glory was short-lived. On returning home I read various derogatory newspaper articles about my jungle experience, and listened to hurtful comments being made about me on a variety of TV and radio programmes. Jonathan Ross on his Radio Two show, which has around eight million listeners, said I looked so awful I shouldn't be allowed to be seen on TV, and that I should go away and do something about it. Various male writers in a number of tabloids backed up this view. The worst thing was that even though I found opinions such as these little more than an expression of body fascism, secretly I agreed with them.

There seemed to be an obsession about the fact I hadn't worn any make-up in the jungle. The sexes were divided over what I regarded as a quite trivial matter: certain women declared that it was refreshing to see another woman facially naked, while numerous men vocalized their disgust at the fact that an older woman should have the audacity to grace their screens exposing her imperfections. There appeared to be no praise or observations about the hardship endured, and quite frankly I felt that this blanket negativity could seriously damage my career.

This difficult period in my life gave me the determination to seek some sort of cosmetic surgery, which I intended to see through to the end. So I began to pester people – from show-business friends to 'women who lunch' – for the information I required. I needed to know who was the most reliable, talented and trusted surgeon around at the moment. These regular 'inquisitions' around the dinner table and over morning coffee eventually led to me finding out about Botox.

I first learned of its existence through a female comedian I was having lunch with in 2001. She suddenly got up and left the table after our meal exclaiming, 'I'm going to be late for my Botox appointment!' Not having a clue what she meant I had to ask around. This was a treatment that had somehow escaped my knowledge, but it transpired that it had been in use for several years as woman's greatest beauty secret, and apparently everyone in the know was doing it. In retrospect I now realize that certain figures in the showbiz world must have been using it for almost fifteen years because, without naming names, some people don't seem to have aged a day since the early nineties, and their best smile is more of a rictus grin.

The following year, in February 2002, I was on the phone to a journalist, Janice*, who told me that she was on her way to have Botox injected into her armpits. 'What! Why? Are you mad?' I shouted down the phone. 'That sounds like hell on earth!'

'It's what all the Hollywood stars do before the Oscars,' Janice replied.

'Oh, yeah? Does it help them win?' I enquired cheekily.

'No. It stops their armpits sweating all over their hired Armani gowns, so I'm trying it out to see if it works, then writing it up for the paper.'

'It sounds so painful and pathetic; sweating is only natural.'

'I don't really care,' was Janice's response. 'Look, come on. If it works, it's worth a bit of discomfort.'

Can you imagine having needles in your armpits? What's next? Elastoplasts to cover the puncture wounds, followed by the agony of peeling them off? Do we just want to pay for the chance to experience some pain? Are women addicted to discomfort? Wouldn't it be easier to get a lazy, jobless boyfriend who could give us the grief for free?

The specialist who was to administer this small act of torture upon Janice was Dr Patrick Bowler, whom she eventually persuaded me to meet. I was very cautious about the encounter, especially as the only knowledge I had about the procedure had come from the daily newspapers, and also because it seemed to me that the practice sounded like voluntary poisoning. After all, the Botox product originates from botulin, a bacteria that causes food poisoning, but when used in this derivative it appears to have the miraculous effect of 'freezing' muscle. Small injections of Botox are administered to the muscles in the face that cause all our lines and wrinkles. The most obvious areas for this treatment are on the crow's feet around the eyes and on the frown lines of the forehead. By freezing or partially paralysing the muscles that create the frown or the creasing around the eyes, the effect is to smooth the skin on the forehead and the eyes, and prevent the formation of future wrinkles.

Though Botox has been available as a cosmetic therapy for the past twenty years, not enough time has passed to gauge whether there will be any long-term problems associated with its use. Supposedly there are no dangerous after-effects, allergic reactions to the product are rare, and it does eventually wear off after three months. I've heard some people say that it's possible to tell when the effect of the treatment is wearing off because the skin in the affected area becomes dry and appears more lined than before, but of course this can be combated by further treatment.

Patrick Bowler works from Wimpole Street. I was surprised to be met with patience and understanding when I produced a list of questions as long as my arm, having become accustomed to being hurried in and out of appointments. Will I get poisoned? Will it paralyse my face? Could I have an allergic reaction? The answer was 'no' on all counts. I ended up having two consultations before I took the plunge. It was only when I realized that all my friends had been having Botox for years that I thought I was a complete fool for not doing it sooner; ten years sooner, to be precise. None of my friends had told me that they were Botox veterans, not even when I was fretting over my own frown lines. I had my small revenge, however, as Dr Patrick Bowler turned out to be a jewel in the crown of the cosmetics world.

Patrick never hurries; he is calm, deliberate and very considerate. The extent of his professional expertise means that he isn't solely concerned with the business of applying Botox to a rich clientele, as he's also a leading light in the field of dermatology, and is used to dealing with a variety of more serious problems, from birthmarks to aggressive skin cancer. He has an aesthetic opinion, which is vital when administering Botox, otherwise overuse of the product could leave a client with staring eyes and a dribbling mouth. It is my belief that only those people with strong critical opinions about beauty should work with Botox as it really does go beyond the skin – both inwardly and outwardly. Essentially we are all diverse and individual characters with vastly contrasting faces that need to be observed, studied and assessed before embarking upon such a procedure, which is why I had two consultations with Patrick before he carried out any treatment, as it gave him the chance to monitor how I use my face, to see the position of my laughter lines and the movement of my mouth.

One of my main concerns was that as an actress it was critical that I retained the ability to be expressive. I had heard tales from the acting world that directors and casting directors were completely against the use of Botox, and stories had started to infiltrate the business about actresses who weren't able to express anger or sorrow properly because their faces were frozen in smooth perfection. There were even rumours about it being used on the mouth lines with the result that some A-listers have been rendered unable to crack a smile.

This is one of life's conundrums: facial expression and fighting wrinkles are at opposite ends of the spectrum, and so those who want eternal youth sacrifice their smiles, while people like me, who wear our hearts on our sleeves, consequently have our whole lives mapped out in a topographical dance on our face. Luckily it is possible to use Botox to reduce lines while still being able to move the facial muscles, but it means that the amount injected is considerably smaller, and it is therefore necessary to return for more frequent top-ups, which I choose to do, to avoid being stuck with an expressionless face. Some practitioners wouldn't be happy with this, believing that they had failed to give value for money. This may be so, but ultimately it's the customer's choice if they wish to preserve as much of their natural look as possible, especially for professional reasons.

In more extreme and irresponsible cases Botox has been used on the lines of the throat and on rare occasions has caused the client to suffocate. Because of the dangers associated with its overuse it would certainly be wise to avoid 'Botox parties', which are champagne affairs where a practitioner goes around the guests administering the treatment. Equally, popping into an unknown shop at lunchtime is best avoided, unless you have had strong recommendations from trusted friends.

Botox is sometimes referred to as 'plastic surgery without a scalpel' because if it is injected into the muscles above the brow bone, it will lift the whole brow area to produce a look known as the 'LA lift'. It takes an experienced practitioner to apply such a technique; in the wrong hands it's possible to be left looking like a rabbit caught in the headlights for three months, until the effect finally wears off.

Eventually Patrick and I decided what was best for my tired old face. He would give special attention to applying Botox to the area beneath my eyes as the skin had been overly stressed by my enthusiastic use of expression (which I put down to years of laughing too much). This would smooth out the skin, remove the slack wrinkled appearance and help delay the need for surgery until I could find the right man for the job. He would also give me Botox around my 'crow's feet', the outer edges of the eye, to smooth away those wrinkles, before administering the LA lift. Any pain was worth it when presented with the end result. What is a little discomfort from a needle if the final outcome is that you lose ten years of worry from your face?

The first injection of Botox can take anything up to ten days to take effect. Eventually there is a definite sensation of the forehead muscles being frozen, as a lifelong habit of frowning is inhibited for the first time in one's life. It's a feeling that I really like. After the Botox, Patrick went on to freeze my mouth with a painkilling fluid in order to inject Rhestoline into the crease lines from my nose to the mouth; he also filled the vertical lines on my top lip and redefined my lip shape. As women get older, their hormones decrease, and one result is that the top lip becomes thinner in appearance. Consequently, this procedure is a perfect way to improve the shape and look of the top lip. Rhestoline is a man-made 'filler' which mimics human body fat. It can last from as long as six months to two years. For people who smoke, who have to purse up their lips to inhale, it will break down more quickly and the effect won't last as long, unlike mine, which lasted the full two years.

It is possible to have an allergic reaction to this product, which may have contributed to the problems that Leslie Ash has experienced, so it is important that your specialist gives you a small amount in your arm and leaves it for two weeks to be doubly sure that you don't react negatively to it. To me the results were fantastic and gave me so much confidence. I have been seeing Patrick for two years now and the effects are just as satisfactory as they were in the beginning. He has been so consistently wonderful that I happily recommend him to friends.

Yet even these procedures couldn't delay the inevitable for much longer. Exhaustion had taken its toll on my face and no amount of Botox was going to reverse that. When I told Patrick that I was going to go ahead and have a facelift he informed me of all the surgeons who, in his opinion, he believed to be the best, but I must admit that I was nervous about having the operation done in Britain. I had not long returned from the jungle and was still being followed by paparazzi men in white vans (as subtle as piss in the snow), so the thought of them photographing me through the recovery-room window chilled me to the bone.

As well as seeing Patrick Bowler, for the past two years I had also been having my skin 'conditioned' by Linda Meredith at her salon in Knightsbridge. Linda designs facials to suit the skin's needs, which can involve anything from oxygen being pumped into the skin using a high-pressure applicator, to using electrical pulses to tighten the facial muscles, as well as conditioning the skin with natural, organic creams. The result is radiant, healthy skin, which is evident in photo sessions and on screen. It is vital to treat your skin – the largest organ in the human body – as a living, breathing being; we forget all too often that it needs to be nourished and conditioned. Facials and natural skin creams keep the tone of the skin at its peak.

Linda had a lot of clients with the same dilemma as me and so she was often asked if she could recommend a surgeon. As a facial specialist she was bound to see the results of not only the best surgery but also the worst, and so she had amassed considerable knowledge about the subject. Most professionals in the beauty industry who specialize in facial skin recommend that people should resist the knife at all costs, but even Linda admits that there comes a time when one cannot continue to fight the ageing battle without some sort of invasive surgery. 'It's no good, Toyah. You need a little help,' she said to me, one day. I was grateful for her honesty at a time when I still had a chance to do something about it, as I certainly didn't want to leave things until it was too late, and one day wake up to find my chin on my lap.

Linda has good contacts but even she discovered there was something of a closed-shop mentality in existence when enquiring about who's hot and who's not in the world of cosmetic surgery. Names were passed around but no one would admit to having had work done by any of them, and the few that did own up didn't have that 'wow' factor when you saw the end result, in my view. However, one name cropped up quite often in her enquiries – Dev Basra. I had heard of him before, as he had acquired legendary status in the world of reconstructive surgery, especially in the 1980s and 1990s. Even with our combined contacts, neither of us could track him down. We seemed to have hit a smokescreen of confidentiality and just couldn't make contact with him: some said he'd retired, others said he didn't work in England any more. It appeared that he wasn't affiliated with any of the popular and well-established clinics in Hampstead, Harley Street or Manchester; indeed, his whereabouts was completely shrouded in mystery, which was very frustrating as, according to rumour, he was the best.

Continuing in our quest to meet the top surgeons, we hadn't had much luck, until one day Linda phoned me in what can only be described as a heightened state of pure joy. 'I've found the man! He's wonderful! Perfect!' she declared. 'I've seen his book [a photographic journal of his work, before and after] and talked to him about his technique, and do you know what? All his work is natural in appearance, he doesn't give you the "LA stretch", and he hates the surgically enhanced look.'

That day Linda had gone to Claridge's Hotel at the suggestion of a friend to meet a surgeon who was fast becoming the talk of the town. If Linda was convinced enough to recommend this man to me then I had to take her very seriously. As someone responsible for looking after members of the Hollywood and rock-world elite, Linda is on the A-list of beauty specialists, an expert at creating treatments for individuals' needs. Her job is not just limited to treating dry skin, acne and wrinkles, as she is increasingly caring for skin that has been abused by inappropriate products and procedures; in particular, acid peels: 'As the skin gets older why on earth would you want to make it thinner with a peel? Many doctors say that the skin will renew itself through this procedure, but I'm not convinced. Skin gets thinner with age. How thin will your skin be by the time you're sixty if you have regular peels?'

As someone who has had to treat many types of people, including women who have had too many procedures, I trust Linda's opinion above all others: 'I can't believe how these doctors can do this to their clients . . . They only have so many layers of skin, and if you remove too many you are left with skin like paper that can split! It can make the skin appear so delicate and shiny, like plastic.'

Linda has also seen many bad or noticeable facelifts enter her salon. She knows exactly what ageing skin responds to, in terms of different treatments, and that you can only take it so far: 'This surgeon I've just seen, Toyah, understands exactly what it is I have to deal with. He wouldn't dream of doing any of these aggressive procedures if it will affect the patient negatively in the long term, because he has had to do too much "correctional work" from other surgeons' mistakes. He believes all surgery must look "natural".'

Linda revealed that out of every surgeon she had met, she was sure that this man had a true knowledge of how skin responds to different treatments over time. He knew the consequences of having surgery, how the operation would 'behave' in years to come, how long it would last and how the ageing process would effect the operation eventually, so he would make sure that he restructured prolapsed muscle rather than pulling skin tight over the top. In Linda's opinion, he was the most informed surgeon she had ever met.

Dr Olivier Henry de Frahan was the man whom Linda recommended I should contact. (Though his full surname is the aristocratic sounding 'Henry de Frahan', he would prefer to be referred to as 'Olivier de Frahan' throughout this book.) He works from Paris where he operates at a private hospital, and also has a suite at Claridge's where he meets his 'Anglo-Saxon' clientele every two weeks. He is one of Europe's leading plastic surgeons, and although he has made his name through cosmetic work performed on major European film stars, he also has the Hollywood A-team crossing the pond to have undetectable improvements made to their million-dollar faces and perfect bodies. So I booked my appointment, and, carrying my emotional baggage from my troubled past, I went to meet him.

Claridge's is the domain of the super-rich. It made me feel good about myself just walking through the front door. But when I got into the lift to go up to the suite where the doctor meets his clients, I was already in the company of an Oscar-winning director and two international playboys. Fortunately they exited the lift at the floor below the suite where I was heading – it would have been hugely embarrassing sitting in a waiting room with a man who has an Oscar in his downstairs loo, with both of us knowing whom we were going to see and why.

Dr Olivier de Frahan entered the room in the style of a small tornado. He was impossibly tall, and far too thin in my opinion. I could have wrapped my hand around his wrist. My first thought was that he needed a good meal inside him. His English was delightful and entertaining for the first five minutes, but when we got to the point where I needed to unload twenty years of plastic-surgery anxiety, I felt the need to ask him to repeat things to be absolutely sure of what he was saying.

The room in which we met was small, more of a beautician's room than an office. He asked me to lie on a table in the middle of the room and tell him exactly what it was that I wanted done. I told him I wanted a facelift. 'No, no, no, no,' he said, shaking his head. 'You don't need one. You look too young.'

'But I work in television and these jowls are a real problem,' I replied, desperately pointing to the offending area.

He looked long and hard at my face before declaring, 'I can definitely improve your eyes, that is not a problem, but a facelift, no!'

By this point I was almost panicking. I couldn't stand the thought of having one operation only to have to follow it with another a year or two later. I really wanted to deal with this now, in one go. I can't help but feel that there's something really unhealthy about multiple surgery – I don't believe that it's safe to have too many shots of anaesthesia.

'Doctor, my face is hard to light,' I told him directly. 'I'm receiving reviews about my looks and not about my work. I feel very strongly that I have to take some action to improve my face.'

With this he produced a digital camera and proceeded to photograph me from three angles: centre, profile and three-quarter profile. When he looked back at the shots on the camera's screen he was surprised by the results.

'That is unusual. I can see the problem with my own eyes: you have lost the youthful structure and the harmony of your curves around your cheekbones, but you photograph too well. You look good in pictures,' he surmised. 'I need to see the problem to work out how best to take it away.'

'I have photos where I look bad. In fact I have hundreds of them,' I replied. All I had to do was fish out most of the press shots from *I'm A Celebrity, Get Me Out Of Here!* of which none was in the least bit flattering.

So he sent me away with the task of finding photos that emphasized what I didn't like about my appearance. He also needed pictures that explained what I liked about myself, flattering ones that showed off my eyes and jaw line when I was younger.

This first meeting was in October 2003. I liked him immediately. There was an eccentric, intelligent charm about him. He listened to my questions and requests patiently, but it was also obvious he was an unforgiving perfectionist when it came to his work. This is what really decided matters for me. Time was not on my side, however, as I had concerts and Christmas shows for the rest of the year, which meant that I had to free up some time early in 2004. This wasn't going to be easy – agents want their clients to work.

The next time I saw the doctor was two months later in early December. I had decided before the meeting that I was going to go ahead, and I knew when it would have to be. It had to be in late February 2004, which was the only window I could make in my busy schedule.

The reason I had so firmly made up my mind by this time is the same reason I am writing this book. There was a small feeding frenzy when Dr Olivier de Frahan was found. All my close girl friends went to see him and they all felt that he was the man for them. One of these was Linda Meredith, who was able to have her surgery in December 2003, which gave me the opportunity to see the surgeon's work at first hand. It was stunning. But on reliving Linda's journey with her I realized that there are so many questions that need to be asked by those who are giving serious thought to having a procedure, which can only be answered by those people who have been through the experience themselves. A doctor can only tell you so much about how you are going to feel; he cannot inform you of the anxieties that are only natural when you put your life and face into someone else's hands.

This is why and where my diary begins.

On 10 December 2003 I walked into Dr Olivier de Frahan's Claridge's suite with a pile of photos from my past and we discussed the possibility of how certain elements of my youth could be recaptured. After much debate he agreed to give me a lower lift, which would involve making an incision from the top of the ear, down around the front of the ear, all the way around to the back of the same ear where the cut would go into the hairline, allowing him to reposition the muscles around my sagging jaw line and to tighten the skin on my neck.

The description made me feel uncomfortable. The reality of it all hit me hard, but the truth is that if you want to look better you have to face a fact that is unavoidable: your skin has to be cut. I realized that despite having done everything possible to remain in good shape over the years – I don't smoke, drink, over-eat or stay up late – age inevitably catches up with you.

With regard to my eyes, the doctor explained that it would involve a simple procedure of making an incision below the lower lashes, right from the inner corner of the eye all along the lower contour to about a quarter of an inch beyond the outer corner of the eye, rather like using eye-liner.

'That's a long cut!' I remarked.

'It will be completely invisible,' he reassured me. 'Below the eye I will lift and reposition your eye muscles, which have slackened. This is a major operation. You will be in surgery for four hours! I take my time, everything must be right. Also the slower I work, the less pain you will have because I am not tearing any muscles.

'I will keep you completely natural; it will be better for you. Everyone knows who you are and how old you are. Believe me, you do not want to look stretched!'

Once I was happy with the technique the doctor proposed to use on me, we discussed the issue of cost. This can vary according to age, skin type and whether you're having follow-up work done on an earlier procedure; for example, if you're having a second facelift the old scar tissue needs to be removed first, which makes the surgery more time-consuming and more costly as a result. His fee was 11,000 euros (approximately £7,500), and if he was to operate in February I needed to pay a deposit immediately, in order to guarantee my appointment.

There was a lot of discussion about the date, as he tends to be booked up months in advance, but he understood that my free time was limited, and agreed to find space to accommodate me. We set the date for 23 February 2004, which was the nearest time to a new moon that he could fit me in. I was too embarrassed to tell him that because I live by the phases of the moon this was important to me. At new moon you tend to bleed less, whereas at full moon there is a greater chance of excessive bleeding.

The commitment had been made – now there was no turning back.

THE DIARY

Today I had my final meeting with Dr Olivier de Frahan before the operation in Paris on 23 February. It was the last chance I had to ask any questions concerning practical matters, rather than the surgery itself. I particularly wanted to know whether I'd need night-clothes in hospital, and also if the doctor would want to see me the day before the operation.

My friend and facial expert, Linda Meredith, who found and introduced me to the doctor in October 2003, was so impressed with him that she booked herself to have the same procedure as me in December, and since the operation is now well on the way to recovery. I have been calling her on a regular basis ever since to find out about her progress and to check on how she is feeling. She is delighted.

But Linda did admit to me that three weeks after the operation she hit a psychological wall and found herself questioning her decision and wondering what the hell she had done, but that feeling didn't last, and now she is in heaven and full of self-belief. Needing to discuss the anxiety I was now experiencing about having my own face cut, I phoned her to ask how she had felt before the actual operation.

'You know, Toyah, I didn't give it a thought,' she replied. 'I was too busy paying bills and getting everything in order before I left, then once I got there I thought, "Damn it! Let's get it done!"'

She went on to reveal that the aftercare she received from the doctor was extraordinary. It filled her with confidence, and made her feel very secure in his hands.

While I was sitting in the waiting room at Claridge's, who should walk in but Linda! It was a complete surprise and such a blessing, as I really needed to see her, to check out the results of her operation two and a half months on, before I took the plunge myself. Not only has her face changed, but her whole body language has too. I was impressed. The Linda I knew before the surgery was a smart practical person, but now I was seeing a woman who appeared to have regained an intense sexual strength. Her dress sense was powerful and dramatic, and she looked stunning. I became convinced that the operation had not only eliminated her very slight jowls and tightened her neckline, but it had also altered her self-perception. She is reinvented. She appeared taller, her posture had changed and the clothes she was wearing reflected her inner confidence – it's as if she had reclaimed a lost energy. Linda was definitely making a statement.

The first thing I did was to ask to see the scars. The cut around the ear was still visible, but only just. Around the back of her head in her hairline there were more noticeable scars that were bright red in colour, but that, she assured me, was because a red antiseptic was used on the skin during the operation, and the hair (for she was shaved behind the ears) was already growing back and soon all would be covered. It was only ten weeks since the surgery, however, and it wouldn't be long before the scars disappeared altogether. Even now, the visibility of any scarring was minimal, far less than I expected.

I walked around to face her and she looked wonderful. The lines of old had gone, and her neck, which wasn't that bad in the first place, now looked like that of a twenty-five-year-old. The results were so good I felt confident that I was doing the right thing. Even so there was still a knot in my stomach. I felt terrified. I told myself that if I was this nervous after seeing the results of the surgeon's work with my own eyes, then I'd just have to accept that I was going to be nervous for the whole journey.

The problem I had was that even though Linda's scars were neat and super fine, I really didn't want to see any evidence of a scar at all, which was completely impractical, as time is needed to complete the healing process, for such scars to disappear altogether.

Dr Olivier de Frahan came out to say hello to us both and I congratulated him. He took Linda by her arm and lifted up the back of her hair to explain the process he would be carrying out on me, pointing out that the visible scar at the front of the ear would vanish completely.

'You see this line, Toyah?' he said, indicating the scar at the back of Linda's ear. 'I lift the spare skin from the neck and hide the scar in the hairline. It is like making a dress, no? I put the pieces together.' I couldn't help but think that none of the dresses I've ever made has needed so crucial a fit.

Linda was so pleased with the outcome of her operation that if any of her clients ask about surgery not only does she recommend her surgeon, but she also shows her results to those who are interested. Not surprisingly they are excited about it because it means they have direct access to Linda's experience, and can see the work up close, which is exactly what anyone considering surgery needs – the reassurance of seeing a good result for themselves.

I told Linda that I was keeping a diary of all the events building up to my operation because I was finding it quite distressing that there was a distinct lack of people with first-hand experience of the procedure to whom I could talk, who could have told me a great deal and eased some of my worries. I also asked her if she minded me revealing that it was she who had discovered the surgeon, though I promised not to say that she had had the procedure herself. Her reply was not only refreshing, but it gave me a much-needed confidence boost concerning the writing of this book: 'Tell them! I tell everyone who comes into the salon whether they want to hear about it or not! I'm proud of what I have done, and I think Dr Olivier de Frahan has the right ethics. He keeps his clients looking natural – he doesn't just stretch the skin, he restructures the muscle, and he wouldn't carry out a procedure unless he thinks it is totally necessary. No, you put it in your book; I don't have a problem with that at all.'

I felt a great sense of relief, firstly because Linda looked fantastic, but also because her openness about the subject mirrored my views exactly.

I've had conversations lately that have baffled me. I've been at dinner tables where I've announced, 'I'm going to have surgery. Does anyone think I'm bonkers?' and to my relief everyone has been supportive. Indeed, later in the evening, individual women have spoken to me privately and revealed that they have already had surgery, and are delighted for me that I'm going to do the same. Unfortunately they haven't the confidence to talk openly about it because they've been too embarrassed. One friend took me aside and said that her husband had not only paid for her boob job, but he had also found the surgeon who carried out the procedure. Her main problem had been that as a result of having children earlier in life her body shape had changed, which left her so ashamed of her breasts that she had no confidence about 'being on top' during sex. The resulting surgery changed their sex life and saved their relationship – now she's on top all the time!

Does this beg the question that breast implants are a male conspiracy to get the girls 'on top'? The tragedy is that she still finds it difficult to admit it to her friends, not so much that she has had the op, but more to do with the fact that she would have to admit to being imperfect in the first place. I've heard this type of story so many times. It is all too common. I even have one female friend who goes off in secret to have procedures such as Botox and lip implants done without telling her husband. Though he has never noticed, she feels better about herself. When I asked her why she never told her husband she was shocked: 'He mustn't know. He must presume I am perfect, naturally!' She has the right to her secrets, of course, but I feel I also have the right to speak.

All these comments have come from naturally beautiful women, each of whom I've told they had nothing to worry about, particularly when compared to some of us who've had to make love 'on top' wearing Damart vests and a paper bag over our heads since we were thirty, as *our* husbands hadn't offered to find or pay for a surgeon . . .

MONDAY 16 FEBRUARY 2004

Even after having seen the positive effects of Linda Meredith's operation, studying her minimal scars and realizing how happy she is now, I was still over-anxious about it all, especially the operation itself. Sleeping has been proving difficult, as I've been worrying about the possibility of the scars around my ears being abnormally visible, despite the fact I had seen the results of the doctor's work, where the cut was minimal, and had been reassured that any scarring eventually disappears. This so concerned me, however, that I would cancel the whole operation if necessary.

Twenty years ago I remember doing a photo-shoot with a very famous hairdresser who had what looked like white, raised, serrated scars running down the sides of his ears. His heavily orange tan did little to hide the vicious-looking scars, which could easily have been mistaken for a 'DIY' face job. Now I am frightened of the same thing happening to me. I don't want people to realize that I've had surgery through noticing any tell-tale scars. As I get older I find it bad enough that very few people actually look in my eyes when they talk to me, as if the signs of ageing on my face are too unattractive to view directly; I certainly don't want people looking at my ears during the course of a conversation, staring in horror, smirking at the subtle signs that indicate my misplaced vanity. In a perfect world I want people just to see me, to recognize the light behind my eyes and notice that I've taken care of myself over the years. Is that too much to ask?

To a lot of people cosmetic surgery has always been intrinsically linked to social status, and it occurs to me that by having a facelift I could conceivably be closing the door on ever playing the role of a suburban checkout girl. Or am I? My trip to Paris is costing approximately 15,000 euros (about £10,500), including the price of hotel and travel, but if I were to go to South Africa or Hungary or even Russia I could have the same operation for a third of this price. People from all classes are now able to afford this type of surgery, and so I can still play a suburban checkout girl because plastic surgery really is available to all who are willing to pay for it and many, many people are; perhaps most surprisingly, the suburban wives and husbands of middle England.

Throughout the morning I was able to dismiss most of my fears myself, but by 11 a.m. I needed the support of others. I phoned Jon Roseman, my media manager, first, but didn't quite get the response I was expecting.

'How much do you want for the story?' he asked.

'I don't want the story to get out!' I replied indignantly.

'Listen, everybody is going to know because you're going to look different.'

'Not *that* different!' I replied. 'OK, so I'll be having a complete makeover with hairstyle and clothes all changing once I've had the op, but I won't look so different that my skin is as smooth as Joan Rivers's.'

'Look, you've worked your arse off for God knows how many years, and now you're doing something to give yourself another ten years in the business,' he said, encouragingly. 'You should be proud of yourself. *I'm* proud of you. There's nothing wrong with what you are doing – it's a life choice, so be proud of it. Anyway, everyone will know eventually, so how much do you want for the story?'

Well, I had called him for his backing, and I reckon I'd got it.

All my close friends are right behind me; from Danniella Westbrook to my blue-blood, feminist friend Veronica, who I thought would shout me off the telephone when I first told her. Instead she offered to come and look after me once I'd had the surgery. Their support came as a huge relief. I didn't feel that anyone was laughing behind my back, in fact, quite the opposite. Everyone seemed wildly excited and couldn't wait to see me afterwards. Interestingly, all my friends who work with television presenters thought it perfectly natural and wanted me back at work as soon as humanly possible.

All my actor friends were supportive, but secretive. I knew for a fact that I was going to a surgeon who had operated on actors from Los Angeles to Israel, firstly because Paris is a great place to hide, but secondly because this guy is the best in the world for giving his clients a natural look; he keeps your uniqueness so that you don't come away looking like Cher's half-sister. I think this is why so many American stars are increasingly heading to Paris to have their work done. It is the European style to keep everything natural, something far removed from the LA stretch. When talking to the actors I know who I have since discovered had been to Dr Olivier de Frahan themselves, they are supportive but do not admit to having been under his knife, and have simply said, 'Oh, he is the best! He does everyone. All my friends have been to him.' This reassures me, and at the same time tells me that in the acting world no one admits to it, but they are all doing it.

By lunchtime I am a completely different person. I must have phoned a group of about twenty very different people, from casting directors to vicars, and I haven't had one negative reaction. A weight has been lifted off my shoulders in the knowledge that I have the unswerving support of my friends.

For the past three years I have been close friends with Martin Gold, a northern comedian whom I met while starring in a Christmas show in Stockport. He drives a flash car with his name on the number plate, dresses in Armani, has very white teeth, highlighted hair in the style of Nicky Clarke, a permanent tan in the manner of Dale Winton, is rarely seen without a glamorous girl on his arm wearing a fur coat of the *Coronation Street* camp, lives with his mother in a Leeds mansion he built himself that makes Dame Barbara Cartland look cheap, and has a deep, almost unfathomable, northern accent.

He is humorous not because he is a comedian by trade, but he's funny in spite of himself. He has the most traditional male attitude towards women I have ever come across, in that they should be beautiful, ornamental, good cooks and good in bed, or in his own words, 'The cooking's not important; we could always eat out.' The vainest fashion victim in the world, he has a heart of gold and a gob like a dumper truck, though not because he swears, because he doesn't; in fact his morals are higher than a mountain and he won't entertain sleaze or swearing. No, his mouth is like a dumper truck because of his delicious lack of tact and the fact that the verbal holes he digs for himself could reach Australia.

We often spend days in a state of complete hilarity in Harrods in Knightsbridge just laughing at the price tags. He's there because he likes to be seen there, I'm there because I get a thrill out of seeing the rich burn their money. On one occasion, in 2003, we almost got asked to leave when we cheekily asked an assistant whether a rhinestone wastepaper bin – with a price tag of £3,000 – came with the glass display cabinet in which it was contained.

I love his company. Why? Because my deliberate lack of ostentation truly horrifies and disturbs him: 'Toyah! You know I always avoid going out with you on the fifth of November in case people throw money at you! You're loaded, so why don't you dress appropriately? Make more of yourself.'

'Because, Martin, there are poor people out there struggling to buy their week's worth of food and I don't want to walk around like an idiot in designer clothes. I think it's insulting. Wealth does not "maketh" the man,' I respond. The truth is that to me money is a commodity that should grow, not be thrown away by the gullible and the bored.

'Toyah, I've been poor and I've been rich: rich is better. You're a travesty, you could do so well for yourself,' was his uncomprehending reply.

Sometimes I think Martin is actually ashamed to be seen with me. Soon I was to find out why I get this feeling when I'm out with him. I decided to give Martin a call because I like him, and I trust his response will not hide his true feelings – he is a great truth barometer. Furthermore, he happens to know lots of people on the cabaret circuit who have opted for the knife. In fact, they have all had some cosmetic procedure not because they needed it, but because to them it's a sign of success.

'Martin, I'm having a facelift,' I said, during the call. 'Do you think I'm wise?'

There's an audible sigh of relief on the other end of the phone. 'I was just saying to my mother the other day – we were watching you on *Stars In Their Eyes* – I said to my mother, "Hasn't she looked after herself well? Good shapely arms, fantastic bum. She has a great body, she's fit, she's talented, and even has a nice face if only she'd do something with it. The bags under those eyes, and they're not even Gucci!"'

That was a compliment, believe it or not, but at least Martin had answered my question for me. I adore Martin Gold; he might be vain but he isn't pretending to be anything else. He is the true northerner who would be there to catch me if I ever fell, but I want him to know I will never, ever buy a fur coat!

The last call I made was to a female agent, who manages film and TV actors. On her books are all the current soap stars – she deals with the bright young things and the golden oldies from *EastEnders* to *Coronation Street*.

'The thing is, Toyah, you look amazing,' she began. 'Not when you were in the jungle – you looked pretty awful in the jungle – but I couldn't believe how good you looked on stage when I saw you at Christmas, fabulous in fact. I couldn't take my eyes off you. Even up close you look younger than your years, with great skin and great eyes, but for TV you've got no choice. Do it!'

Most years I invest in a new house or a painting. This year I'm investing in myself and, I hope, my future.

THURSDAY 19 FEBRUARY 2004

At 6 a.m. I woke up from a dream in which I was trying to climb down from the very top of a church tower while wrestling in my head with intellectual snobs who were laughing at me. If that wasn't enough of a paranoid soup to find myself in early in the morning, I swore I could feel phantom pains around my ears, as if I'd already had the operation.

There is a clamouring of many different reasons, excuses and possibilities screaming out in my head and I wish to God they'd shut the fuck up! This is stupid. Why? Because I know that once I get to the hospital in Paris I will be as cool as a cucumber; it's the waiting that's so bloody torturous. To date I have done everything physically possible to prepare myself for this apparent act of madness. I have been thinking of, dreaming of, saving my pennies for and expecting this day to arrive since I hit twenty-six years old – the age of no return. Part of me is loving this journey, for many reasons: financially, I can afford it; it's a damn good excuse to take a month off work; and at the end of it I expect to be able to continue my career for a good ten years with a face that matches my energy levels.

Even my husband has said it's a good investment. Bless him. He has never once questioned my judgement on this. We've been married for nineteen years, and consequently he's fully aware that he hasn't got a cat in hell's chance of changing my mind, so he might as well support me. For the past fifteen years he has had to put up with me stretching my skin tightly across my face with my fingers saying, 'If only I could look like this!' Now the time has come for something to be done, and perhaps he's relieved that my nightly mirror contortions will finally come to an end. There's a far more obvious reason Robert is so cool about this, though. He's a musician, a guitarist and the founder member of the band King Crimson. He has worked with some of the most beautiful women in the world, and knows perfectly well what the pressures of appearing youthful are like. Knowing he has recorded with Blondie, whenever I see press articles where Debbie Harry admits to having had three facelifts, I run to him screaming ecstatically, 'If it's good enough for Debbie, it's good enough for me!'

Not only does Robert spend the majority of his time in America, the plastic-surgery capital of the world, he has a sister, Patricia, who has lived in San Francisco since the late 1960s, and is one of America's leading public speakers. She holds conferences for super-companies from Microsoft to NBC to Coca-Cola, and has won countless awards in a tough, male-dominated industry. It is her responsibility to motivate the workforces within these huge conglomerates to achieve higher annual targets in order to compete effectively with rivals. Patricia's work is far from easy; sometimes she can find herself being flown to Australia for a day's meeting, on to England for a lunchtime speech and then back to the US for a seminar in Las Vegas. Her feet hardly touch the ground. This type of work demands that she and her fellow speakers must look pristine, from the clothes they wear to their entire physical appearance. During one of my many phone calls to her I asked her if she ever felt the pressure that I was under, because even though she has not had surgery, a lot of the people in her line of work have.

'Many male and female professional speakers in the USA are investing in cosmetic surgery, because many of our clients and audiences are years younger than we are,' she said. 'They hire us for our maturity and wisdom, but we want to look young enough not be discounted as "over the hill".'

Patricia is in her fifties and proud of it, but she has always looked twenty years younger. She runs marathons regularly without any fanfare or fuss, and is the one person I know who has inherited good genes. The two of us are very similar in that we are blessed (some may say cursed) with the physical energy of a hyperactive ten-year-old who's just drunk a bottle of orange pop. Our energy just doesn't fit our age, and makes us appear freakish to those who prefer a more sedentary lifestyle.

It is fabulous for me to be able to talk to someone who has witnessed the results of so many cosmetic-surgery procedures among her work colleagues. I can ask her about things that I'd be afraid to ask the surgeon, such as whether the surgery scars should go in the ears and be hidden from view. I've discovered that they can and they most commonly do in America, but it depends on the cutting technique the surgeon chooses. I wonder why mine won't be hidden in the ears, as the cuts that will be

In my youth, people always commented on my flawless skin (*left*) and, of course, my outrageous costumes (*below*).

As my career took off, I was constantly on the road touring. But the gruelling regime began taking its toll almost immediately – here I'm just twenty-six, yet the wrinkles under my eyes are already well-established (*left*).

Above: Acting alongside Katharine Hepburn in *The Corn Is Green* (1979). Even this Hollywood icon was continually judged on her appearance, suffering the most appalling abuse about her looks from the moment her career began until it neared its end.

Below: In 1979 I played the part of Miranda in Derek Jarman's *The Tempest*.

Top: Performing as Sally Bowles in a stage version of *Cabaret* in 1987. As I grew older, I still felt as sexy as I had done playing this sultry role, yet the rest of the world seemed unable to appreciate it.

Left: A seasoned pantomime performer, in 1994 I had great fun playing the title role in *Peter Pan*.

Facing page: Playing the title role in *Calamity Jane* was the part of a lifetime, but the exhausting run left me with even baggier eyes and more wrinkles than I could count.

Facing page: Competing in *I'm A Celebrity, Get Me Out Of Here!* in April–May 2003. The programme was the final straw for me, with the media delighting in commenting on my worn-out-looking face and lack of make-up (*top*). Me with John Fashanu in the jungle (*centre*) and hugging Danniella Westbrook as she leaves the camp (*bottom*). We've since become close friends, and Danniella's advice on my surgery – coming from one who has had several operations herself – was invaluable.

Above: It was a great relief to be reunited with my husband Robert after my Australian jungle experience.

By now the evidence of my age was impossible to ignore – in every picture I saw of myself I looked older than my years and I was seriously unhappy with my appearance: it simply didn't match the feisty and energetic person I knew myself to be.

made to my face are going down the sides of my ears, the thought of which is causing me to have sleepless nights. My surgeon has explained that to put the scar in the ear is a dead giveaway, as it distorts the small piece of gristle in the centre of the ear, and sometimes even flattens it. He described how you can often tell a facelift done in LA because this part of the ear is distended. He prefers to put the scar in a natural crease line that runs down the front of the ear. I do trust him, and I value his judgement and experience. In fact, rumour has it that he has just worked on the Italian prime minister and a supermodel, so I'm fully aware that this guy is good. I am simply verging on a nervous breakdown through the worry of it all, and becoming a neurotic fusspot.

Patricia was surprised that I was having a lift at the age of forty-five, as she thought I was far too young and that I should wait perhaps until I was fifty. But she fully understood why I felt the need to go ahead with the operation, possibly more so than some of my British friends. Having lived in the US for thirty years, she is surrounded by women who have had surgery. On the West Coast particularly, it is almost a crime to age gracefully there. Even among some of the most staunch feminists the scalpel is seen as the symbol of feminine choice, a 'fuck you' to all the clichés and insults that attach themselves to women over the age of forty; women who are perceived as having lost their sexual power, which is an image first thought up and perpetuated almost exclusively by men.

That apart, what I really needed to know from my sister-in-law was whether I could still wear ear plugs after the op, as Robert snores like a dinosaur with wind.

'Er . . . No. Definitely not!' she replied. 'You might come undone!'

I was also concerned about post-operative constipation, as operations tend to cause this due to the effect of dehydration during the surgery, so I also wanted to know from Pat, 'After the op, if I strain when I go to the loo will I damage my face?'

'Now you're being stupid, Toyah,' Pat replied, in her pronounced American drawl. 'But take some syrup of figs with you.'

So that's yet another item for the shopping list. The chemist must think I have the worst case of piles in history, as so far this week I have been to the pharmacy every day to buy a list of items that could soothe nasty cuts on the face as well as clear up unpleasant things on the bum: arnica ointment, tea tree oil, vitamin E, cod liver oil, Hypercal ointment, hemp oil, iron supplement without yeast, vitamin skin cream, acidophilus capsules and a packet of drinking straws. The straws are the only things I am worried about carrying through customs, mainly in case I'm suspected of having a heavy coke problem. I really do need to bring them, however, as I don't know how I'm going to feel about swallowing after the operation, and I'd rather be prepared than not. But if they enquire, how do I explain the situation to customs officers who are hell bent on finding illegal drugs? 'Oh, an entire pack of drinking straws, sir? Well, I anticipate I'm going to have a very sore throat for most of the week. And the suitcase full of alternative therapies? That's for my piles!' That response should do the trick, and also, I hope, reduce my chances of being body-searched. One of the good things about being older is that customs men suddenly lose all interest in conducting body-searches on you. In my punk-rock days we always had to add a couple of hours to our travel itinerary for the obligatory strip-search – they'd find any excuse in 1981.

By 7 a.m. my husband had stirred from the land he inhabits in his sleep that is oblivious to the sound of his foghorn. How people can snore the way they do and not make themselves permanently deaf is something of a minor miracle.

There wasn't even a hint of light coming through the window at that time in the morning, only darkness. Winter is still very much with us. Our home is in the depths of Worcestershire and I feel very safe here, but there is a growing weight in my stomach and I've become aware that I've been developing a certain 'neediness' of late. I've reverted to a childlike state inasmuch as I've begun clinging to my husband in an uncharacteristic way, but Robert has said he likes this and could get used to it. Vulnerability may be an ever present part of my psyche, but normally I would never, ever show it. Now it is seeping guiltily from every pore.

Later in the day we cuddled up on the sofa in our living room and I told him that I hoped I wouldn't drive him mad next week, particularly if I whinged and had sleepless nights. He nibbled my left ear and laughed, saying, '*I* won't be able to do that next week.'

I suspect he's looking forward to a whole week of me being in an immobile state. Whenever we visit Paris I usually encourage him to walk ten hours a day, and so the thought of seven days of hotel food, a good book and unlimited time at his computer is probably putting him in seventh heaven.

FRIDAY 20 FEBRUARY 2004

Waiting! Waiting! Waiting! Time is going so slowly, too slowly, and now it is driving me crazy. I'm wishing desperately that I'd already had the op so that I can hurry up and get on with the healing process.

I've been lucky enough to have spent this last month at home, as I'm usually touring or filming TV programmes in London. Admittedly it has been a hectic four weeks involving the reassessment of all my business deals, which have been a little neglected over the last couple of years while I've been on the road. I've also spent time building new ideas for the future, which required my full concentration and commitment, but equally I've had the chance to recharge my exhausted body after two years of back-breaking slog. Now I am in a physical condition strong enough for surgery, but I'm bored of waiting and the thought of another month at home recuperating after the op doesn't exactly fill me with glee. I like challenges from the outside world and I'm now getting withdrawal symptoms. There is nothing like an offer of work from an unexpected source to give me a spurt of creative energy.

A new emotional pattern started today; in fact quite a few different feelings emerged. I'm aware that I don't want to be on my own and I find myself following Robert around like a wounded pup. Also I keep going from moments of great confidence to tearful fear, and so I'm getting a sense of how testing I will be as a patient next week.

SATURDAY 21 FEBRUARY 2004

I kept myself in a state of artificial busy-ness today, in particular finishing off the shopping so that our main home in Worcestershire is stocked with provisions when I return. Once I'm back from Paris I won't want to go out shopping for food, as doubtless I'll be very self-conscious about the visible stitches on my face, so I've made sure the cupboards are topped up with tomato soup and chocolate, which I'm definitely going to need. Even as a keen detox devotee, chocolate is a vice I'll never give up fully. Sometimes my craving for the stuff is so bad I would happily walk round to the shop naked but for a bunch of flowers up my backside if that was the only option I had, so it's a good idea to have plenty in the house. It occurs to me that our home in London will need stocking up too as I'll go back there first when I return to England.

While loading up my car I told Robert I'd meet him in London later tonight to prepare for our journey to Paris together on Sunday. He had to drive to London separately as he needs his own transport for travelling to and from the airport on his frequent trips to the US.

My stomach was in my socks at this point. Leaving home had never been so difficult, especially knowing that I wouldn't see Robert for a good six hours. Oh, unhappy me! Robert is my security blanket.

I have two riverside cottages a mile down the road from my Worcestershire home. One is my hideaway, the other is where my parents live. When I dropped in to check that all was safe and well, and to say goodbye to my parents, I fought off the urge to tell my father what I was about to do. Robert and I have successfully deceived my parents into believing that we are going on a nice long holiday. As my father is eighty-three and my mother is seventy-six, I thought it would be utterly irresponsible to tell them I was going to another country to have major surgery, so as I shouted goodbye to them from the car I told them I'd see them in a week or two. I don't like telling lies and to deceive one's parents seems terribly disloyal. My father, in his grand octogenarian state, has taken on the characteristics of a wise and faithful lapdog, whose doleful eyes could persuade money out of even Gordon Brown's pocket. It is hell not telling them the truth, especially my dad, but I do think I'm doing the right thing.

On arrival at my London home I began cleaning the house from top to bottom, which wasn't a huge task as it's only a one-up one-down property. Cleanliness has taken on a whole new meaning to me, as apart from distracting me from worrying thoughts, it is also necessary for maintaining my good health. When I return from Paris I will be more susceptible to infection, so I had to make sure that every surface was bleached. I even prepared the garden for the spring. I completed all of these tasks in a trance-like state of numbness. It was as if I was trying to work myself into a state of exhaustion so that by Monday, the day of the op, I'd be so tired that I'd sleep for a week. Though I am clearly in conflict with myself, the will for surgical enhancement is still stronger than the will to grow old gracefully.

Two hours of frantic cleaning later and still no resolutions had been reached in my head; there was so much internal dialogue going on up there it was like a W.I. meeting on speed! Robert arrived at about 6 p.m. and I was gladly distracted from my niggling thoughts. We went out to supper and returned to watch DVDs in bed, and then sleep.

SUNDAY 22 FEBRUARY 2004

All was calm this morning, but it was very cold; the early spring has been usurped by the dispossessed winter.

Tomorrow is the big day. I'm so numb with fear it feels like each of my limbs has been removed and stuck back on with Play-Doh. Robert and I did our final packing together. As I'd realized that fancy clothes were pointless, I opted to bring very little with me, but my computer and a good read were a must; in fact Clive Barker is always a must when convalescing. It helps to read horror stories about other people's lives when you look like one yourself. I'd chosen *Coldheart Canyon,* a nice yarn about a movie star who has a botched face job, murders his surgeon and has to hide in the Hollywood Hills. That should put a smile on my face at three on a sleepless morning in Paris!

After having had many debates on the subject of privacy and about not being recognized on my return, we decided that a private jet would be too expensive and the risk of being spotted by the media at a major airport was too great, so in the end we chose to go by Eurostar. I have a small phobia about being photographed by the paparazzi looking a complete idiot, all bandaged up, black-and-blue, stapled together and swollen. If I was discovered in such a state it wouldn't exactly aid the healing process, especially when recalling how the press vilify women who have even the most basic of procedures, such as my friend Leslie Ash. Then of course there was the worry that my operation could go wrong, Oh, for goodness sake! Someone put me to sleep – I'm going completely doolally!

Robert and I stood baffled in the middle of Waterloo station as all around us commuters were seemingly able to make sense of the system of message-board mayhem. As my pre-op stress built up, I was slowly becoming hopeless at practicalities. I couldn't even sort my return ticket from my outward ticket, and I held up the queue at the entrance barrier for ten minutes in a blind panic. At this stage Robert, who understood exactly what was happening to me, kicked into superhuman gear and tried to calm me down. Eventually a kindly guard approached us and explained where we had to put our tickets – I had other ideas, like a rail executive's mouth, perhaps – and eventually we both made it to our seats in first class.

Once on the train I could settle, and I buried my head in the *News of the World* to read about the naughty things that fellow celebs had been up to this week.

Paris arrived quickly and at last I became resolute about my decision. A strange calm descended, and I felt as I do when I'm watching snowflakes falling through the silent air.

Our hotel is perfect and not at all commercial; in fact it looks more like it was once the private home of some French aristocrat. It's on the edge of the city, in the hospital district; the Arc de Triomphe is a ten-minute walk away and the clinic where I will have my operation in the morning is on the next street, in the 16th Arrondissement. The doctor had told me he wanted me close to the hospital so he could keep a close eye on me while he continued his other surgery during the week, so thank you Dr Olivier de Frahan for organizing my stay in a perfect, security-gated private establishment that was used by Madonna on her European tour. It has two large ornamental security gates to keep the world out and the guest in. The only embarrassing thing for me is that everyone who stays here is beautiful; jet-set to be exact. By tomorrow I think I will be staying in my room for the rest of my visit.

The doctor had given me the choice of three hotels in the area: a cheap one, an average one and an expensive one. A friend reminded me that on an adventure such as this, one should not be cutting corners and that I should treat it as a holiday of a lifetime. So in the end I opted for the expensive hotel, and as it turns out, the doctor had negotiated a price that is a gift.

I methodically unpacked and took out all the things that I thought I'd need post-op, putting them within easy reach of the bed. I'm guessing that by the time I return to this room on Tuesday I will not be in the mood for doing much walking around. Our room is fine; it's big enough for me to pace up and down in the night if I cannot sleep, and is certainly big enough for two single-minded people to share.

Afterwards Robert and I did our most favourite thing: we donned our sensible shoes and walked the streets of Paris, hand in hand. My hands were clammy. If Robert hadn't been here with me I know I would have been a complete wreck. He commented that he had never known me to need him so badly, so desperate am I for his physical presence and his strength. In turn I had never known him respond so fully to my needs before.

We looked for a place to eat. I wasn't that hungry but we found a superb Lebanese restaurant and went in for a vegetarian feast. We were the only people in there. I looked across the table at my hubby and I loved him so much for tolerating my vanity. Food was a good distraction, though I only had until 10 p.m. and then I wasn't allowed to eat or drink till after the op.

I realized that Parisian life could entertain me for hours and hours while we 'people-watched' out of the window, the rain falling gently. As we listened to the music coming from the restaurant speakers, European rock songs were telling stories of angst and broken hearts in many different languages but always relating the same pain. Then, completely out of the blue, 'The Rose' came on, sung in English. This is a song I have sung many times on *Songs of Praise* (for my sins), and the show is always deluged with requests for it. In fact it has become so popular to those who follow my career that recordings of my version of the song have even been played at loved ones' funerals (it is odd to think that I could have a second career as a funeral singer). It is a song I take very seriously as every time I have performed it the occasion has marked a milestone in my life, and now there it was, totally unexpected and in English among all the other foreign languages. At first I just pointed out the coincidence to Robert and we listened. I hadn't heard the song for a year. Then the notes took their fingers and opened up my heart, as good music always does, and in front of countless passers-by on the rainy streets of Paris I sat in the restaurant crying and crying, all the month's tensions melting into tears. After wiping my face and blowing my nose, I thanked the angel who protects me for being there with me in the room that night.

MONDAY 23 FEBRUARY 2004

Well, here it is, the day that has kept me awake for the past two weeks – the day of the operation.

If it were physically possible for a human being to wake up while encased in a block of ice, I did it this morning. The fear was lurking under the surface of my skin, but it was there all the same and I certainly didn't want to show it to Robert. The thought of him having to suffer most of the day after leaving me in tears kept me from cracking.

I have done everything I possibly can to make this day perfect in timing, as well as safe, because I have timed it to the new moon. The doctor had even moved one of his patients to fit me in as close as possible to last Friday's new moon. Why a new moon? Well, apart from the fact that most of my astrological chart and personal influences relate to that phase of the moon, a new moon symbolizes new birth and new beginnings. It is also widely believed that a person will bleed less at a new moon. Consequently I would never choose to be cut open around the time of a full moon as any bleeding that occurs could be harder to stop. There is no scientific proof to back up this viewpoint, probably because if there were, operating theatres around the world would be forced to shut down on the day of a full moon! If I really had to fight my corner on this judgement I would point out that for centuries farmers have followed the cycle of the moon to govern when they plant and when they reap, and as for the tides that rule the earth's great seas, is anyone going to argue that the moon doesn't influence these?

You are forgiven for thinking I'm a little mad, but I did consult an astrologer about the timing of the operation and whether I should have a facelift in the first place. Thankfully I was assured that everything was favourable. It is not something I would usually do, but when you're about to put your life and your face in someone else's hands I believe you should be bloody thorough and cover every piece of ground. One point my astrologer did make quite earnestly was that the moon on Monday 23 February would be in Aries, and so she wondered whether it was possible for me to move the operation to Wednesday when the moon would be in Taurus, which is my own sign. I explained that I had already had to pull a rabbit out of a hat to get this appointment, as my surgeon had a six-month waiting list and I could not mess him around any more. At this point she told me that the moon in Aries meant that accidents were more likely to occur, so it was up to me to ensure that all was in order when I went into the operating theatre.

This information distressed me at first, as I'd expected to be unconscious before entering the theatre, and I couldn't imagine asking the French surgical team to double-check that their equipment wasn't faulty and to sharpen their scalpels. But then she put my mind at rest and assured me that it all bodes well for the future. 'It looks like being a success,' she said. 'Next year is all about new beginnings, new opportunities, and they are all linked to your image.' I am not so gullible as to swallow up this kind of information literally; rather I believe that it acts as a barometer for the influences that surround me, influences that I really take seriously. Some bad days are painted in your astrological chart in Day-Glo colours, so it would be stupid to ignore them. Luckily for me, this isn't one of those days.

I also timed the day of my op to fall after my period. I'm as mad and as bloated as a goldfish on helium during my cycle, and always too hormonal for comfort. I have been detoxifying now for two months, which means no Diet Coke (I can drink a litre of the stuff a day), no coffee, no alcohol and no tea. I've been restricted to fresh fruit and vegetables, and on top of that I've been taking a natural iron supplement and following a course of detox supplements created by a man called Joshi.

Joshi is the detox guru to the stars. I first met him six months ago while working on *Calamity Jane*. I was in a state of advanced exhaustion and in order to get me through the rest of the show's run he immediately put me on his detox programme to help my body eliminate all the stored toxins, which, in effect, had been dragging me down to 'below par'. I had to cut out all processed foods such as white flour and white sugar from my diet. All my caffeine treats had to go too, including Diet Coke and also chocolate, which contains a surprising amount of caffeine. Joshi supplies you with supplements made up from a secret herbal remedy that improves the body's ability to purge toxins. This means you pee a lot, poo a lot and sweat more than normal, but it's worth it because the detox is so efficient: it improves the liver's function and therefore your immunity is boosted, as is the body's ability to heal itself, which is absolutely crucial if you're about to have major surgery.

I was awake by 5 a.m. and lay in bed looking at Robert while he slept. Again and again it kept running through my mind that I could not go through this without him being here. I was terribly thirsty and equally as hungry, but as I never usually eat or drink until after sunrise, it had to be psychosomatic because I'm not allowed to consume anything until after the op.

This morning I was in no mood to talk and was trying desperately not to let my fear of the unknown betray my true feelings. Robert and I left the hotel very early. The street was deserted and the air felt pure. No cars passed us as we made our way to the clinic, a small private hospital where I would be having my operation. I saw it for the first time last night from the outside, when Robert and I returned to our hotel. It looked crisp and white, not at all like an English hospital; a small, purpose-built, modern-looking building where the rich come in secret to fight the signs of ageing, and where super-experienced surgeons forge their way into a future where age as we know it may one day be eliminated. So it was there that we found ourselves again, hand in hand and trusting that this was all going to be OK.

When we arrived it was 8 a.m. and I was bewildered with emotional exhaustion. Our breath was visible in the air and my lungs were stinging. I was freezing. I couldn't even be bothered to dress smartly for the occasion. It had taken all of my strength just to arrange myself in a tatty black parka, a big wrap-around scarf and trainers on my feet. In my right hand was a bag with a nightgown to cover my one-night stay, as well as a picture of Robert. In my other hand I carried the results of my blood tests and the ECG for the anaesthetist to examine before I entered the operating theatre. I had dressed for tomorrow, because tomorrow I knew I wouldn't give a damn how I looked. I was an hour away from the operation and still questioning myself about whether I was doing the right thing.

Inside the clinic I found that I wasn't the first in reception. Sitting nervously in the corner of the room were two women, obviously friends, in the national dress of Parisian *mesdames* – large brown fur coat, impossibly high stiletto shoes for impossibly narrow feet – but wearing no make-up and looking as sick with fear as I felt. Without the make-up they both looked about fifty years old, but with it they could have probably fooled a stranger into believing that they were all of forty-five. I could tell that they smoked, as they had those smoker's lines etched from the mouth to the nose to the eyes. No doubt they have cursed the day they first lit up in much the same way as I've rued the fact I've probably laughed too much; we all carry our wrinkles, but for different reasons. Anyway, as I continued waiting, they were led away to whatever torture they had chosen to liberate themselves from their advancing years.

Because I was completely incapable of conversation I sent Robert away with a hug and a kiss, telling him I would be fine. As he walked away it dawned on me that the next time I would see him my face would have changed for ever. Will it be good, will it be bad? Is this the point of no return? I was past caring. I was too damned tired.

Sitting there all alone I realized that I was almost completely surrounded by whiteness. White walls, white flowers, white uniforms, presumably to promote the building as being super-clean. Not one nurse passed me with blood smeared across her white overalls, which was a relief.

I was called into a side room to fill in some forms and leave my credit card in the safe. Really, as if I'd do a runner once I came round. It was a fabulous thought, though. Robert could have a car waiting and once the surgeon had spent four hours miraculously and brilliantly recreating my face we could simply disappear back to England without paying!

The forms were basic address, next-of-kin stuff, but they were to be filled in directly on the computer. The receptionist didn't speak English and my little knowledge of French was cowering in fear at the back of my mind. I think that I shouldn't have sent Robert away because at least he has the confidence to *pretend* to know what people are saying. Now I felt panic rising. Will I be sent away if I cannot communicate my details? I tried to solve the problem by writing everything down for the receptionist, but I noticed that she was typing it incorrectly into the computer, so eventually I went over and filled in the form directly on screen myself, which was a relief to both of us.

After that the day's events proceeded at breakneck speed. If things hadn't moved along swiftly, it would have cruelly prolonged my suffering, so I was truly grateful that the hospital had to keep to such a frantic timetable. Either they were giving me no time to mull things over, change my mind or run away, or they were simply being bloody efficient (I suspect it was the latter), but within five minutes of completing the computerized form I was in my own private room. The name on the door was 'Emerald' (which incidentally is my birthstone), and the room number was 'eight', which happens to be the Feng Shui number for good luck. I felt like phoning my astrologer there and then and telling her, 'Hey! I'm going to live! I'm in room number eight!'

The room was typical of a private hospital room, and just large enough for the bed, a heart monitor and a television. A few steps away there was a private bathroom, but I didn't have much time to take everything in as a nurse arrived and asked me to undress and put on a green gown; one of those sexy things that doesn't do up properly at the back. Luckily the nurse was heaven-sent as she had good English and was brimming with sympathy and support. Then, just as quickly, the anaesthetist arrived. Communication-wise I was virtually back to square one with him as he had very little English, though just enough to understand my fears. Before he started going through my medical history he gave me a pill to relax me, which gave me the chance to have a much-needed sip of water. Not having been able to drink any fluids since 11 o'clock the previous night, I was as parched as a desert rat's gonads.

I tried to explain my fears to the anaesthetist and I prayed he understood. At this point I should confess something about the main reason behind the blind panic I've had for the last two weeks: during an unexpected bout of illness sixteen years ago I developed a phobia of being put to sleep. In my younger days I had been fitted with a coil, which later became embedded in the wall of my womb, possibly as a result of my three-hourly gym sessions. I'd had an infection of the womb and bowel and became seriously ill, needing three operations in one week. After the last operation, I had problems coming round. It was while trying to regain consciousness that I had a very strange experience where I developed out-of-body awareness. I still had my physical sensations, and I knew I was choking, but I could also feel that I was standing next to the bed watching myself. Looking over me were two nurses who kept staring at me lying in the bed saying, 'She's having problems,' while from the side of the bed I was shouting back at them, 'My trachea is blocked! I can't breathe!' but of course they couldn't hear me. At this point I sensed myself running into the hospital corridor to seek help, but of course I wasn't 'solid'. Eventually my body coughed and this brought me back into my normal self. I'd had an out-of-body experience where I could hear with great clarity but also see when I was clearly unconscious. When I was properly awake I repeated the conversation word for word, which really stunned the nurses.

I didn't go into all this detail with the anaesthetist today, but I did explain that I was worried about my breathing becoming restricted when I came round, and I also mentioned that as a singer my throat is very sensitive. He understood and dismissed my concerns, assuring me that anaesthesia techniques have progressed significantly in the past sixteen years; they are less aggressive and so I would be given only the minimum needed to keep me under. I was hoping he'd mention the tube that goes into the trachea as soon as the patient is unconscious (which I'm sure caused my choking episode), and that he would tell me he would be extra careful. But I realized he has to get in there immediately and get me breathing on a ventilator, so I stayed quiet and assumed an air of confidence.

When the anaesthetist left I told the nurse who would be with me through recovery that I have a tendency to get very cold. Though she must have heard countless patients nervously rattle through their pre-op fears, she was absolutely wonderful. She listened and understood, and told me not to worry because she would be there with me. All this was in broken English, of course, but when you're at your wits' end and feeling as though you're about to be turned inside out from your derrière upwards with anxiety, every two-syllable word and mimed gesture that cross a great gulf of possible misunderstanding are all gratefully received.

By 8.30 a.m. I'd only been at the hospital for half an hour, but already the theatre trolley had arrived for me. Standing there in my green paper gown that did nothing to lessen the feeling of nudity, my feet in matching green paper socks, I lifted myself onto the trolley. This was it. I was harbouring excitement. I always knew this moment would come. From the second I turned twenty-six, when I felt my body reverse from being young to growing mature, a switch flicked and I changed from admiring myself in the mirror to observing the transformations of age.

As the trolley was wheeled out of the room my heart began to race. Thoughts like 'It's going to be four hours until I'm awake – do I want the toilet?' were rushing through my head. In a few moments I would be entering the place where I really wanted to chat to people at every opportunity to ask about how much pain I was going to experience when I came round. Although this would be my last chance before waking up after the event, I really wasn't sure whether I could ask those last remaining questions. The language barrier would still be a problem, of course, but even if anyone were able to answer my queries in English, they would only be able to speculate; it was for me to find out.

The hospital wasn't that big but my journey on the trolley took me to a lift, down two floors and through a corridor that appeared to be lined with people in green overalls, then on into a small, 10-by-11-foot operating theatre, brimming with humming and buzzing machinery. My eyes took in every detail: the heart monitor, the tubes from the wall that carried the vital gases, from oxygen to nitrogen. Everything had a sparkle to it as the light was so bright.

As soon as I was placed on the operating table I started to shake. I couldn't help it. It wasn't the cold; I was just shitting myself. Each member of the team bent over to say hello and gave me reassuring smiles, which offered me some comfort.

The anaesthetist busied himself setting up my drip. At first he tried to put a needle into my right arm, but my veins collapsed on penetration. I've always had this problem, and I warned him that it has taken some people fifteen attempts, testing their patience until they tire before they go for the back of my hand, leaving my arm looking like a pin cushion. He seemed to understand my explanation, but fortunately had better luck with my left arm. Yes, I'd make a rotten junkie.

I couldn't read the anaesthetist's mood. Upstairs in my room he was friendly and direct, but down in theatre he seemed to have shifted into a different gear. I felt he was a little tense, but as I was already on medication, I was in too vulnerable a condition to deal with it. The sedation was certainly adding to my confusion, but it did feel like he was pushing the needle into my arm as if he was trying to give a small mouse multiple stab wounds. I decided not to react, and didn't even flinch. He walked around the operating table and tried to lift my left arm out of the neck of my gown, but the neck was too tight and my arm became stuck, so he ripped the gown instead of cutting it with scissors, which left me feeling exposed. I sensed the nurse's irritation with him while she gently covered me up.

A drip was attached to my right arm. 'Your breakfast!' laughed the anaesthetist, and he pointed to his throat, saying, 'It will stop you being so dry.' I suspected he was an impatient man rather than a man of wit. Unlike everyone else in the operating theatre he seemed to have little time for nurturing nervous foibles. But he was right, the drip instantly relieved my dry throat and the urge to cough stopped immediately.

Dr Olivier de Frahan's assistant sat beside me. Her English is a hundred times better than my French and she explained to me that she had decided to get me into theatre early because she felt it would help keep me calm if I could see my surroundings. She was so right. After what my astrologer had said about making sure all was in order, this gave me the perfect opportunity to do so, and I asked her how she thought I would feel when I came round. She assured me that the pain control these days was so advanced that I would experience very little discomfort. As she continued to keep me calm, I tried to look at the instruments that would be used during the operation, but they had wisely been kept out of sight. With my astrologer's words ringing in my ears I told myself it would be absurd for a scalpel not to be sharp enough. Surely that would be impossible? The doctor's assistant treated me and all my questions with great sensitivity, as did the nurses who constantly squeezed my hands to give me much-needed reassurance.

It was 9.30 a.m. when Dr Olivier de Frahan arrived to mark my face. This was something he would usually do in the hospital bedroom, but because his assistant had insisted I should see the theatre before being put under, the usual routine had been changed slightly. When I had met him for consultations in London he was always professionally attentive but aloof. Here he was focused and serious, but like everyone else in the room he was showing considerable tenderness towards my state of anxiety.

He entered the room like a small hurricane and the calm, relaxed atmosphere was instantly transformed into 'operational mode'. Everything and everyone were immediately focused around him; his every command heeded by worker ants responding to the man at the very top of the tree. He was wearing green overalls like everyone else, his wayward hair kept in place under a green cap. His arrival made me feel safe for the first time; his authoritative air wasn't pompous, but truly justified. It was obvious that everyone in the room was excited to be working with him; I imagined that it was probably like getting the chance to assist Bailey the photographer or Michelangelo the sculptor – everyone felt privileged to be in his company. My nerves soon started to calm.

The doctor began to stick pictures of me on the theatre walls like a fan, which I loved, and I smiled to myself (which was something I wouldn't be doing again for quite a while). I'd supplied him with photos past and present, wanting him to see how my jaw line used to look. Throughout our consultations he had taken photos of my face from every angle and these shots went up on the wall too. As I watched him go about his work, it felt good to know that the recent photos he'd taken would be consigned to the bin once my new face emerged.

He sat beside me, observing me directly for the first time since entering the room, and a look of surprise registered on his face. 'My goodness! Your hair, you look so different!' The last time he saw me I was platinum blonde, but because I didn't want to be recognized by anyone en route to Paris or during my stay, I'd asked a friend to dye my hair brown the week before. It made me look completely different, but it also meant that the incisions which were due to go into the hairline would be disguised by the darker hair colour until they had healed, otherwise they would have appeared bright red through the blonde hair and been a lot more visible. I had also taken a tip from some American friends who advised me that when they had their facelifts they always changed their hairstyle, so when people asked them why they looked so different they could say, 'Oh, I've got a new hairstyle.' Notice the plural there – 'facelifts'!

For a while he continued to look at me with deep concentration. I didn't want to interrupt his flow of thought, but there was something I was desperate to ask him. Eventually he said, 'I keep you very natural.'

I took the opportunity to ask: 'Could you also do my upper eyelids while you're at it?' As I'm here and I've gone through emotional hell to get here, I thought it was worth mentioning. He might as well do the lot because I have no intention of coming back in a hurry, in fact it might be a good idea to make me as tight as possible so it lasts till I'm ninety-nine.

'No. The eyelids are perfect,' he replied, without a hint of humouring me.

'Well, please get rid of my nose-to-mouth line,' I

suggested, knowing full well that if he did this procedure it would require a certain amount of stretching the skin.

'I will keep you natural. I will lift here,' he said, brushing my lower eye area. 'You have wrinkles. All that will go smooth.'

For the first time in the long journey I had made to get to this point, I was starting to think whether I should insist on something more obvious, more stretched, particularly as the whole reason I was here was to get a younger look.

'You don't want to look all pulled. You would look a fool. I will not make a fool of you,' the surgeon assured me while looking over to my pictures on the wall. 'People know who you are, and they are used to your face. They know your age too, so I will refresh your image.'

Of course he was right. He wanted me to return to the workplace to 'work', and not face ridicule from all quarters. He then turned his attention to the task in hand and I didn't speak to him again. I fully trusted his aesthetic judgement and knew he wouldn't leave me looking like a vain idiot.

As he bent over me while scrutinizing my face he said, 'I saw a picture of you on the Internet last night. You look like a model for Thierry Mugler. Very strong.' He was referring to all the way-out images I had had in the 1980s, with the striking make-up and hair, which were photographed by the great beauty photographers John Swannell and Terence Donovan. At least he knew why I had to maintain my looks.

I realized he had carefully examined the photos I'd given him and had concluded that he should give me a natural look based on who and what I am today, not on who I was. I could tell by the way he was studying my eyes that he knew they had always been my strength. Photographers had always focused on the strong contours of my eyes and now the doctor was seeing how he could reinvent them.

He turned my head and, in an unhurried manner, started to brush the hair at the back of my neck very gently, creating various partings to make way for shaving off an area of hair, using what looked like a Bic razor. This made me laugh. He moved on to the other side of my head, and apologized for doing so, saying, 'It will all grow back.' I had known this would happen and I didn't let it bother me.

A nurse passed him a large bottle of pink fluid, which he began to pour all over my hair, while brushing it away from my face. I could only imagine that it was some sort of disinfectant. It was cold and made me shiver even more.

The time had come to proceed. The anaesthetist returned to my side with a huge syringe of white liquid and he attached it to the needle that he'd set in my left arm earlier. Slowly pins and needles crept up my arm and into the back of my throat. The sensation made me feel as if I were rising from the bed, and on the one hand I was thinking, 'How wonderful this feeling is,' while on the other I worried, 'Will I wake again?' Then I was out before I could even wish the doctor good luck.

* * *

I came round without difficulty, and had no problems regaining consciousness, nor any out-of-body experiences. As I woke up and realized that all was well, the relief shot through my nerve endings. Then I vomited.

On regaining consciousness I had no idea of the time or how long I'd been under, though I had been told the surgery would take about four hours. My first memory was of being sick, which happened twice in quick succession, and I guessed it was a combination of the tube coming out of my throat and the tranquillizer I had swallowed before the op.

'Pardon!' I said with every heave. I could hear great amusement in the room and felt a bowl being placed against my lips to catch the fluid. With every retch I kept repeating the word 'Pardon', and a friendly hand would squeeze my arm. I couldn't see and I could hardly hear, as my head and eyes were bandaged.

In reality I was too stoned to care. I was either still heavily drugged from the anaesthetic or dosed up to the hilt on painkillers. There was no discomfort, only exhaustion and tremendous relief to be back in the world again. I knew who I was and where I was. Sensing that it was better to sleep, however, I floated off as quickly as possible. Part of me had decided days ago that when I came round all I would do was visualize a rapid, successful healing, and as I slipped in and out of consciousness I held an image in my head of how I wanted to look, picturing the scars evaporating and myself emerging radiant and laughing.

The relief I felt after discovering that I wasn't in excruciating pain made it possible for me to surrender to sleep. My head was completely wrapped, which wasn't the best thing for a claustrophobic, but the reassuring hand on my arm told me all was as normal as could be expected, so I drifted away quite peacefully.

I slept and slept till Dr Olivier de Frahan came in with the nurses and removed the bandages from my eyes. I said 'Hello' and fought to stay awake. My sleep had been dreamless and I liked it that way. He asked if I was in any pain and I replied that I had no pain at all except in my right foot, which was in agony, and apparently throbbing.

'Your foot?' he asked, slightly bemused.

He turned to the nurses and told them what I had said and they laughed.

'Which foot?'

'My right one.'

They paid it great attention and discovered that it was indeed swollen. After much amazing detective work we all came to the conclusion that it must have been banged in the lift on my return from theatre. I found it quite bizarre that after four hours of complex reconstructive surgery the only thing that should hurt was my right foot. Before the surgery I had applied a support bandage to my right knee – having been born with a twisted leg my right knee dislocates if it is moved inappropriately – to remind everyone not to twist my leg when they moved me from one trolley to another. Whenever I lie down, however, my right foot always twists itself to the side of the bed, so I suppose it was bound to get crushed somewhere along the line!

The doctor checked his work and told me he'd see me in the morning. I fell asleep again.

Later on the night nurse came by and introduced himself. He had limited English but that didn't stop me from guessing he was gay. (I don't know why but when I'm feeling vulnerable I'd much rather be nursed by a gay man than anyone else.) He was deeply apologetic because the doctor had ordered him to put cold compresses on my eyes and then bandage them up for the night. He tried to explain that he wasn't sure why it was necessary because the doctor had never asked for this before: 'I don't know why, but the doctor knows what he wants.'

I didn't question this and I certainly didn't protest, as I knew I had to sit out any kind of discomfort until my face had healed. I think the doctor had known full well that the skin around my eyes needed extra attention and care.

'So I give you half hour, then I return to do it,' the nurse advised me.

Before he came back I took the opportunity to get up, pulling my mobile drip along with me, and teach myself to navigate a path to the bathroom with my eyes closed. This suited me fine as I felt it was far from wise to look in the bathroom mirror. In fact I was dreading seeing myself, knowing it was not going to be a pretty sight for quite a while.

Once upright I felt more wounded than I had when lying down, but it was my right foot that hurt the most; I couldn't even stand on it. They must have used me as a battering ram to get me out of the lift and back into my room.

Sitting on the loo I had my first pee of the day. My head was gently swimming and so I grasped the window sill beside me to stop myself from crashing to the floor. I could have asked for assistance, as there was a panic button by my side, but I felt too shy. It was dark outside and I guessed it was probably about 9.30 at night. I had managed not to look in the mirror as I passed by, but as I sat on the loo trying to make my head stop spinning I saw my reflection in the glass of the window. I looked like a nun with toothache, a chipmunk in a green gown. The window spared me the finer details of the swelling and the stitches under my eyes.

With closed eyes I navigated my way back to bed without stubbing a toe or spilling the drip before another nurse arrived and told me that I had to eat. Unbeknown to me, Robert had popped in to check on me during the afternoon and left me an enormous apple. Laughing and holding it up in the air, the nurse told me, 'I'm hiding this! It could do you damage!'

It hadn't occurred to me that not only would it be almost impossible to open my mouth, but also my throat was as raw as flesh burning in hell. My jaw had been clamped open for four hours and the breathing pipe inserted for just as long, which is obviously what had caused the soreness in my throat. After attempting to open my mouth I realized I could only open it about one centimetre; the hinges of my jaw were stiff and sore. My ears were also raging with white noise, like tinnitus, which I put down to the fact there must have been pressure put on them throughout the operation.

Everyone who came into my room offered me tea and they were all amazed when I declined. Judging by the amount of times I was offered a cuppa they must have been under the impression it was an English addiction. All I could manage was natural yogurt and honey, which slid down my throat like a long-lost lover's tongue coming home. I asked for some ice cream, but the nurse looked shocked and insisted against it. Apparently the coldness might have sent me into shock and my facial muscles could have had an adverse reaction.

Then the male nurse came in with a huge syringe that he attached to the permanent needle in my left arm. 'Antibiotic to stop any infection – you are vulnerable,' he informed me. 'I'm so sorry, I cover your eyes now.'

I really didn't like it. Although the thought of staying this way for ten hours made me freak a little, it would have been too easy and unfair to get ratty with him. He applied cold compresses to my eyes then wrapped a bandage over the top, around and around quite tightly. I persuaded myself that I had to make myself sleep through this. It was happening for a reason and I must not bugger it up.

For a while I sat bolt upright, wondering if I could call Robert and get him to come and say hello, but it would have been impossible to find the hotel number. I didn't know it by heart and so I could have ended up dialling anyone on my mobile by pressing the wrong buttons. Imagine if I'd got through to my parents? There I'd be, mumbling away about not being able to get an apple in my mouth. The only thing I could do was to sleep.

TUESDAY 24 FEBRUARY 2004

Having been asleep for most of the previous day, I think I was awake by about 5 a.m. this morning, but I was still swaddled in bandages and hadn't a clue.

Now that I knew the layout of the room, I got up and did some gentle exercises. If anyone had looked round the door they would certainly have got a surprise. There I was in an open-backed, green gown, drip attached to my left arm, head and eyes bound, doing ballet by the bed – modern ballet, of course – in the national costume of cosmetic surgery and as wobbly as a jelly. Still, there was no pain and last night I'd declined to take painkillers as they can really bugger up the stomach lining. It's not always a wise choice, though, because pain management is about not allowing the body to suffer if the potential for pain is there, and so if I had been in pain this morning it would have been difficult to numb it straight away.

The only discomfort I experienced was sensory deprivation, though perhaps this is too strong a term as it's linked with torture, and this situation was a luxury I had saved for. But with my ears and eyes subdued by the bandages I kept thinking 'What if there was a fire?' Or if a naked man came into my room I wouldn't be able to see him and that would be heartbreaking.

Eventually my ballet steps began to bore me, but I was still feeling surprisingly energetic. As a stroll around the building was out of the question I decided, for a bit of fun, to find my way to the loo and back. That filled all of four minutes. I returned to bed and tried to visualize myself looking stunning and happy, which was quite a hard thing to do when I'd grown so used to the lines on my face.

The drugs had worn off and time was dragging.

Eventually, after what seemed like many hours, the male nurse returned and removed the eye bandages. He'd brought with him a bowl of ice and a pile of cotton pads, and asked me to keep the cold compresses on until the doctor came. It was only 8 o'clock in the morning. I must have been awake for ages.

Now that the operation was over it felt like I had passed a major hurdle. I felt extremely well and rested, and after twenty-four hours I could see again. It was a lovely feeling as I looked around the room bright-eyed and ecstatic at having done something I'd been promising myself for the last ten years. The air on my eyes stopped me from feeling enclosed, and I was filled with childlike excitement at the thought of leaving the hospital and getting back to the hotel to be with Robert.

AAAAAAAHHHHH! I want to go to the hotel *now* and do things!

Breakfast was yogurt again. My throat was really sore. It wasn't an infection, just the effect of friction from the tubes. Thankfully it was the only discomfort I had.

Sweetpea (affectionate slang for my husband) texted me to ask: 'R U READY TO SEE ME?' I found out how confused I was when I discovered that I couldn't work out how to use my phone. All my practical memory had gone, having been blitzed out of my brain either by the drugs or the shock of invasive surgery. I couldn't function in a co-ordinated manner at all. The phone was in my hand and I was pressing buttons, but gibberish was coming up on the screen. I began to get frustrated because I was desperate to see Robert. I hadn't seen him for more than twenty-four hours, and I wanted him to know that I was OK. Eventually I managed to spell 'YRS'.

He appeared around the door.

'I'm confused!' I bleated, and I waited for him to kiss me. In bending over towards me, however, he soon realized that my many bandages posed something of an access problem, and so he stopped and blew me an air kiss instead, before walking around the bed in wonderment. Coming up close to my face he remarked, 'You look good already, your eyes are fabulous.'

I'd never expected this sort of support; at best I imagined I'd receive a resistant, slightly repulsed, reluctant acknowledgement of my discomfort, but Sweetpea seems completely absorbed by the whole event. I think he was possibly enjoying it all.

We laughed about the apple he'd brought in for me yesterday and he took some photos, telling me he had come in to see me when I was unconscious yesterday.

'Didn't that upset you?' I asked.

'No, I took pictures,' he replied. 'You looked really sweet.'

I had asked Robert to keep a visual document of every moment and at every stage of the events in Paris. It doesn't bother me at all to be photographed in this way because I know I'm in an imperfect state. I would feel more inhibited if I were in a posh London studio done up to the nines and trying to be glamorous. Like Robert, I am experiencing a morbid enjoyment of all of this. It feels incredibly real, and above all else there is a certain ridiculousness about it that makes us laugh. He helped me get to the bathroom.

'Who am I? I'm so confused.'

'Now wash your hands. Don't look in the mirror!' he cautioned.

But I did. It wasn't too bad. I resembled a puffer fish that had woken up in a human body. The cuts around the eyes were a bit bloody, and the stitches were blue and looked like badly applied mascara, but there was nothing to cry over.

During the night my eyes must have swollen and I was convinced that there was something poking in them as they hurt and they scratched. I persuaded myself they were internal stitches and I would just have to live with it, though I found it was less painful if I kept my eyes closed.

Eventually Dr Olivier de Frahan arrived. I was itching to leave the hospital to get going with my recovery. After telling him about my eyes hurting, he looked at them closely.

He turned to the nurses and said something, and they replied, 'Non, non.'

It appeared that the stitches around the bottom of my eye were far too long and as my lower eyelids swelled they had turned the stitches inwards, which had caused them to poke directly into the eyeball. With steady hands the doctor snipped them close to the skin and I felt most relieved.

With great care he unpeeled my head like an orange: 'Good!'

My hair had set rock solid from the fluid that the doctor had used in theatre, and it had stayed in exactly the same position it had been throughout yesterday's operation. I felt like an Egyptian mummy that had been excavated after a couple of thousand years. My gravity-defying hair stood tall and proud, and from out of nowhere an image of Stan Laurel suddenly sprang to mind.

The doctor proceeded to inspect his work and tell the nurses what he had done. My room became a mini-masterclass as appreciative members of the nursing staff gathered and complimented him on his great work. He seemed over the moon with the results, and so he should after keeping me in theatre for four hours.

There were some strange sensations going on as he fiddled behind my ears. He didn't say what he was up to, until at one point I heard a pop and experienced a pulling sensation, then a suction sound, and I said 'Oh!' in surprise.

'Sorry, it will feel strange,' he told me. 'I'm removing the drainage tubes from behind your ear.' They must have been submerged beneath the skin and about two to three inches long judging by the sensation of pulling and dragging under my skin as the doctor worked to extract them.

In truth I could not feel a thing, but then he took up a needle and thread and warned, 'I'm sorry, this will hurt,' before proceeding to sew up the hole. I braced myself for pain, but there was none; just the tugging sensation of the needle entering the skin and the thread dragging through. All in a day's work of trying to perfect oneself.

'All normal?' I asked.

'All normal! No walking up hills and no exercise and no straining of any kind, just rest,' he advised me. 'You must not raise your blood pressure because if you burst any blood vessels the internal bleeding is very bad news. You must rest, understand?'

I more than understood. I'd made it this far and no matter how much I wanted to go for a jog and do 400 press-ups I was going to have to resist the impulse. All I wanted was a wholesome square meal and a jaw that would open wide enough to let me say 'Feed me.'

I was rather hoping I would be free to make my exit at this point. There was no great swelling and no overnight dramas, so I asked whether I could pack my apple and nightie and leave? Yes, I could go, I was told, but not before my head was completely wrapped again. It felt huge! Both ears were padded with huge wedges of lint and a long stretchy bandage was wrapped round and round my head and under my chin, pushing my lips out into a fishlike pout.

'You free to go now. I call you later about seeing you tomorrow,' said the doctor.

All the time I am fighting confusion. I've been pretending to be normal, to understand all I am being told, but the fact is that I'm telling my body to do one thing and it's doing the exact opposite as if I've been rewired in the night. I cannot think of phone numbers, cannot read words, and when I try to work out whether to look left or right, my body disobeys me. I'm completely dependent on my husband to make all decisions for me.

Meanwhile Robert had been standing outside so he'd been spared the gory details, which was just as well because so far all he had thought was that I looked cute, and he was happy that I wasn't in any pain.

The big worry I had had about this trip was that I might get ratty and start throwing tantrums. I thought that if I was in pain or frustrated, or if anything went wrong, then I might take it out on Robert. We don't have and have never had the type of relationship that's based on rows, and I didn't want it to start now. However, the experience seems to be bringing us even closer together. He is tremendously sensitive and takes the initiative, and appears to be delighted by the whole event. Because of this I am relaxed and we have so far done nothing but laugh at the ludicrousness of it all and how hysterical it is to be turning into an old fogey. We both creak in the morning, and our grey hair is getting the better of us, but it all seems highly enjoyable at the moment. Doubtless we'll feel very differently in twenty years' time.

It was lovely to walk out of the hospital room. I used my credit card to settle the account with the receptionist, and could have sworn that I saw her wince when she looked at my eyes, even though she must be used to seeing women in a similar state every day. Then Robert and I walked back to the hotel, which took about ten minutes.

I'd wrapped a huge scarf around my bandages and so Robert referred to me as the Elephant Man for the rest of the day. I felt terribly embarrassed walking down the street looking like this. It wasn't a pretty sight and I didn't want to upset anyone who was squeamish. Robert was completely cool about it, however, and thoroughly enjoyed guiding me around the dog mess that veneered virtually every piece of pavement – it was like playing hopscotch while balancing bed linen on your head.

Everyone we walked past seemed to be ignoring the fact that my head was the size of a small planet. Then Robert pointed out that we were in a hospital district not unlike Harley Street, and everyone around here had seen it all before, so I needn't be ashamed of my unusual appearance.

Back at the hotel, as we walked into the reception I put my head down and ran for the room. I didn't want some rich beautiful person knowing what I'd been up to in a desperate attempt to hold off the ravages of age.

My throat was still sore, but remained the source of the only discomfort I was experiencing. There were also some new sensations for me to get used to. I felt as if I were wearing an Easter bonnet, not just because of the bandages but because my neck had been tightened. It felt like a thick elastic band was running under my chin. I liked it though. It made me feel taut and well-secured.

I still couldn't eat. All I'd had in the past forty hours was yogurt with honey. Robert had stocked the room with salads, fruit and Lebanese cakes that smell of rose-water. Delicious! But I couldn't open my mouth as my jaw was stiff and my throat was too sore to swallow anything. The one thing I could fit into my mouth, I discovered, were Pringles crisps because of their flat shape, so I started the slow process of pushing them into my mouth, one by one, and sucking them. (Have you ever tried to suck a cheese-and-onion crisp?) Sadly I couldn't chew; it was too painful.

I spent the rest of the day settled in bed with ice-cold compresses on my eyes, still without any major discomfort.

At every opportunity Robert was taking photos. Normally I loathe being photographed as I find it quite invasive, but here I took a perverse pleasure in it because the shots were slightly morbid. I don't want to forget this experience, as it's the weirdest thing I've ever done. I don't think I'll be going through the pictures in four years' time for memory's sake or that I'll ever be showing them to friends over the dinner table, though they're far more interesting than glamour photos. This is by far the most extreme adventure I have ever had and I'd be a fool not to document it.

WEDNESDAY 25 FEBRUARY 2004

I managed three hours of sleep last night. Sitting up was the only way to achieve it, as the bandage was thick around my head and I didn't want to put too much pressure on the staples at the back of both my ears.

Another reason for choosing not to lie down was that I was worried I might swell up in the night, so I slept in a sitting-up position in the hope that any excess fluid would drain away from my face. Any swelling will put a strain on the stitches, and is definitely best avoided. The lack of sleep didn't bother me; I felt it was more important to keep putting ice-cold compresses on my eyes to reduce the swelling and to draw the bruising out. Miraculously I hadn't swelled up too much, but the bruising under my eyes was deepening in colour all the time, and had now turned a deep saffron yellow.

I kept getting up and just walking around the room simply to kill time and also to stop my body getting weak from inactivity. I must have done this for anything up to two hours, while looking out of the window to see if the sun had risen. At five in the morning Robert was gently snoring. There is no way I could have done all this without him. I would be frightened if he wasn't here.

The most surprising thing for me in these past three days is that I've become very confused. I don't know what day it is, what time it is, how to spell, read or add up numbers. When I try to write, everything comes out backwards. I am actually spelling words backwards, as if some wires have been crossed in my brain. Despite this I feel quite recovered and I'm pleased with how my face is progressing. In fact I'm more than pleased, I'm overjoyed, and it's only two days since the surgery. However, my confusion is getting progressively worse.

My healing is my main priority at the moment, that and the fact I want to see a therapist who will apply lymphatic drainage massage as soon as possible. Lymphatic drainage is a must, but as it is such a precise art it has to be performed by someone specialized, especially when the patient is recovering from a surgical procedure. After facial surgery the lymph glands can store excess water, and so it takes gentle massage to reduce the puffiness, as well as to encourage the lymph glands to drain the facial area. All this has to be done without disturbing the restructured facial tissues, which is crucial.

My bandages were changed again today and I was relieved at being able to feel most of my face as I thought it would be completely numb. Only my ears lacked any sensation. I was still scared to look at the scars there. I thought they were down the side of my ear and because of the numbness the actual scar area felt enormous, though I was sure it wasn't.

The doctor said that I am not through the worst of it yet. In fact the next seven days are crucial because of the risk of haematoma (a solid swelling of clotted blood in the tissues), as there could be internal bleeding. As a result he will be keeping a close eye on me for the next week. I desperately wanted to get back to England with Robert as soon as possible, because next Monday (in five days' time) he has to return to America. If I don't leave with him before then I will have to stay in Paris by myself and then return to the UK alone. This terrifies me as I can only find my way to the bathroom at the moment. Consequently I felt really spaced out, but I decided not to say anything to the doctor until tomorrow. He told me I had to rest in order to keep my blood pressure down.

One result of the changing of the bandage today has revealed that I now have a pronounced chin and a tight neck, rather like that of a ten-year-old. Robert was gobsmacked; he really likes it.

After my wounds were cleaned up Dr Olivier de Frahan revealed to me that he was concerned about the skin behind my left ear. He told me that it had 'suffered', but I couldn't get him to be more specific. However he assured me that he would keep checking it until it had healed.

The doctor sent us off to a chemist to get eye-drops, and also acetone to remove the sticky-tape marks around my neck. My head was still bandaged but I no longer had the bandage passing under my chin. My eyes have bruised more and more each day, and today they were dark, but a Day-Glo yellow had also begun to emerge around them. It was the same with my neck, and I look as though I've been strangled. This made me feel deeply embarrassed being out in public and I tried to cover up as much as possible, but we were in the medical area of Paris, so when a woman walked past us in her best office suit with a huge bandage wrapped around her head and no scarf to hide her modesty, I shouted, '*Snap!*' The shameless hussy!

In the chemist the assistant found my appearance – huge head and swollen eyes with stitches that looked like two large spiders had taken up residence on my face – too much to take, and she was practically bending over trying not to laugh. It suddenly felt like an Alan Partridge-type scene when he is being openly ridiculed to his face. Fortunately the humour rubbed off on me and I left the shop in hysterics and hid around the corner, leaving Robert to explain.

After paying the chemist we realized that our cash reserves were running rather low, and worryingly we had discovered that not every shop or chemist took plastic. I rarely carry cash with me and am used to relying on credit cards all the time. Because I suffer from dyslexia and number blindness at the best of times I can't even remember my PIN numbers and so I'm unable to get money out of cash machines in an emergency. When I do carry cash I'm not able to deal with it very well because I can't always work out exactly how much money I've got. There have been times when I've given people twenty-pound notes (thinking they were fivers) to pay a fifteen-pound bill but not had any change out of three twenties. It got so bad that my husband used to count the money in my purse on my return to make sure no unscrupulous shopkeepers had helped themselves to more than they should have when counting out my money for me.

The hotel had offered us a terrible rate for the sterling that we'd brought with us, and they couldn't cash cheques either, but fortunately Robert knew what to do. After getting me back to the hotel and into bed, he wandered off to the nearest bureau de change, which was a fifteen-minute walk away, close to the Arc de Triomphe, to ensure that our cash-flow crisis was averted at last!

THURSDAY 26 FEBRUARY 2004

At 4 a.m. I woke up and began wondering why the hell anyone would want to put themselves through this sort of experience once, let alone a second time or more! Joan Rivers, Dolly Parton, Cher, Michael Jackson – why? My excuse is that this will be 'just the once', to enable me to work for another ten years in entertainment, a field I love.

I've now had my head in a bandage for four days and I've got to the stage where I really don't like it! I feel trapped. The doctor said the rough patch – the psychological trigger that makes you start to question what you have done – hits most people three weeks after the surgery.

Tonight my lower eyelids were so swollen that they weren't even touching my eyeballs. They were almost pointing outwards and didn't look at all appealing. This is all to be expected though. It's a 'normal' stage to go through after such surgery (if this situation could ever be considered 'normal'). But my eyeballs were dry because of this, and getting irritated by the lack of hydration because I couldn't produce any tears to wet them. I couldn't read or watch telly properly as I wasn't able to focus, and I kept trying to blink. My eyes will close eventually, as the swelling goes down, but for now it's really uncomfortable.

I found myself thinking about the speculation surrounding Michael Jackson, and the fact that his eyes seem to have been cosmetically widened. All I could say was 'Ouch!' He must have to put drops in his eyes the whole time to stop them from dehydrating. I was experiencing discomfort after three days but my eyes will close soon, so I imagine with the work that Michael Jackson has had his eyes may well feel like this permanently. At this present time the thought of having repeated cosmetic surgery reeks to me of a combination of masochism, boredom, having too much money to spend and madness.

My doctor said that he wants me to be bandaged for five days, with the bandages being reduced daily. I can appreciate the need for such thoroughness and caution, because if my blood pressure goes up for any reason I will be at risk of developing haematoma, but all the same this slow healing process is very, very wearing. I think that the fact my head is wrapped has caused me to feel disorientated. My world has shrunk, my hearing and sight affected, and so I think I probably feel worse than I actually am. Despite the bandage situation I am managing to remain in really good spirits. Perhaps because I have got the worst bit – the surgery – over and done with, I'm now experiencing an enormous sense of relief; dry eyes or not, I'm totally over the moon.

When Robert is around (I let him go out as often as possible to enjoy the Parisian air) we spend some time taking pictures of me doing ballet in my nightie, complete with my swaddled mummy's head. These are later e-mailed to all our friends.

My sister Nicola has kept in touch with me constantly and been very supportive. Last night during a telephone conversation she said she wanted her eyelids done for her birthday. She is eight years older than me, but her husband, a world-renowned professor in the field of epilepsy, is adamantly, absolutely dead against it. I'm sure that my sister's phone calls to me to hear about my condition are building a bridge of possibility to enable her to get rid of the genetic 'tired eyes' from which my family suffer.

I woke up again at 9 a.m., as sleep eventually came in the early morning. I recalled feeling weak and giddy last night. It was the first time since the operation that I had felt properly unwell, but lying down seemed to cure it quite quickly. Also I'd started to experience a small sensation of pain around my eyes, but I decided not to take unnecessary medication such as painkillers and sleeping pills because they affect my moods for a long time. I have always believed that pain is a sign of healing and that is what I am telling myself now. The pain I am experiencing is manifesting itself in a series of sharp little stabs, which then remind me that there are deep cuts on my beloved face, and that freaks me out a little. It's because I love my face I've had to harm it. You always hurt . . . Even with all this sensory deprivation and healing twinges going on under the bandages, my state of mind has remained resilient and positive. I'd even go so far as to say that I've wavered between being ecstatic to extremely ecstatic in the last three days.

Because my brain is like mincemeat, I am making myself write in the hope the fog will lift. My appetite has returned a little and I am not revolted by food the way I have been in the past week, but my hunger reflexes are remarkably slower than normal. I usually think about food constantly and whenever we take a holiday food is always a priority when choosing our destination. Now I am forgetting to eat and when I do it is only in minute quantities, mainly because my jaw hinges are still extremely sore and my throat continues to hurt from the operation, but each day these improve.

I seem to need very little to sustain me, and so far, for three days, I have experienced no hunger pangs at all. Since Monday though, I have lost about 6 pounds in weight, which, because I'm only 5 foot tall and usually weigh about 7 stone 13 pounds, is rather drastic. The doctor noticed my weight loss yesterday, and reminded me that diet is critical at this stage. What I do manage to eat is wholesome, however, as the Lebanese restaurant where we ate on Sunday also does excellent takeaway food, and Robert now goes daily to get houmous and salads. I try to eat a banana a day; honey and yogurt continue to go down well. I still have to slice food up into tiny slivers and push it through the meagre opening between my teeth, as I can only open my jaw about a quarter of an inch at the moment.

At 11 a.m. I had the first in a course of five lymphatic drainage massages at Dr Olivier de Frahan's office. He is based in a large suite behind the clinic, which comprises a study, a post-surgery room, and another large room where the post-operative care assistant works on the patients under his supervision. The doctor is rightly reluctant to leave jobs entirely up to other people, as he feels it is his responsibility to oversee everything. As I lifted myself on to the treatment table the doctor was there telling the care assistant what he wanted to have done and which areas she must not touch, then he left to attend to his other clients who were waiting in the reception area.

The assistant was a French lady in her late forties who had excellent English. She stared into my face and asked me when my surgery was, so I told her it was three days ago. 'Très bon!' she remarked. 'You are doing very well, you look superb!'

Like everyone I had met here, she was able to build up my confidence with great skill. I lay down on the massage table and ever so gently she pushed her fingertips into the skin all over my face. This was good for me as I had yet to touch my face since the operation, being too afraid of how it would feel. The numbness and burning heat I can sense near the scar area would be certain to unsettle me if I was to feel it. In all honesty I didn't want anyone to touch these areas just yet, but as the doctor was ever present I was willing to go along with it. Also Linda Meredith had told me herself that this part of the treatment could not be skipped as it was vital for the skin to drain off excess fluid.

Not only was the assistant releasing stored water in the wounded skin around my features, she was also teaching me about how I was going to feel for a few months, and informing me of the different stages of healing and sensitivity I should expect to experience. Surprisingly, I still have sensitivity and can feel my ears, neck and eyes, but the cut area around my ears feels as if it's an inch wide and equally as deep. This is not the case of course. Having been cut with extreme skill it is probably only a fraction of a millimetre thick, but it is the only part of me that seeems wounded. I started taking Hypericum this morning along with some arnica, which are small homeopathic remedies you can buy in Boots or any health-food shop. They influence the body to heal itself: arnica aids the reduction of shock and bruising, while Hypericum helps encourage nerve repair. The latter came recommended by Shaun Williamson's wife, Melanie, who took it after she had a Caesarean section. I had told her that I was worried about getting the 'numb face', which a lot of people usually get after a facelift, but for some reason I have escaped it.

At midday, immediately after my lymphatic drainage session, which lasted an hour, I went to see Dr Olivier de Frahan. He explained that because he had worked very slowly during the four-hour operation (which consisted of neck, jaw and lower-eyelid tightening), there was less nerve and muscle damage.

'Most surgeons work with too much speed and traumatize the muscle and skin, and this takes a long time to recover from,' he told me, as he carefully cleaned the wounds around the ear with antiseptic and cotton swabs. He has insisted on doing this every day since the operation. I think that not only is he redressing the scar tissue, but he is also de-scabbing it. I've heard that to remove the scabs produced from a procedure such as this is the secret to reducing the scar. Each day it has felt as if the doctor, with great patience, has been gently removing the scabs. But equally I could be wrong, because he has insisted that I must not touch or pick at any of the area. I can only guess as he won't give me the full details, and of course I cannot see for myself exactly what technique he has used. I think he is protective of his winning formula. The ingredients for his success are securely locked away in his head and as his clients cannot see him work directly his secrets remain safe.

Today I asked him to clarify his remark about why the skin 'suffers' behind my left ear. I think he meant it is severely bruised. There is probably a technical term for it, but I believe it has sustained a loss of circulation, and so to remedy the problem he applied a clear liquid that immediately caused a dizzy sensation. 'What is that?' I asked.

'It is used in heart disorders to bring blood into the area. I use it when the skin is suffering. You are healing nicely now, but take this with you,' he replied, handing me a bottle of the clear liquid. 'Dab it on the affected area five times a day, but use it sparingly and wash your hands immediately as it can raise your blood pressure and make your head spin.'

The doctor instils me with confidence. He is honest, but not brutal. He is truthful and he expects his patient's ego to be robust. He has spent a lot of time with me every day, even after his day's surgery; in fact, to my surprise he told me he had done six operations since mine on Monday. I thanked him for his time.

'You are in a foreign country, I must look after you,' he said. 'I don't do this for all my patients. My assistant normally does the redressing after the surgery, but you are here for a short time and I must keep an eye on you.'

FRIDAY 27 FEBRUARY 2004

After six hours' sleep I woke up a completely different person. Unfortunately it was only 6.30 a.m., so I decided to wake Robert because I fancied a conversation.

Prod! Prod! 'Do you want to play?' I asked, up close and personal, my wounded eyes staring into his sleepy face.

'No!' He was not impressed and after getting out of bed and putting on some clothes he went off to breakfast, leaving me to read a newspaper for the first time since Sunday. I thought about joining him in the dining room, as the staff here are incredibly discreet and seem to have been well-trained in that fine art of not noticing people whose heads are completely bandaged. I still felt like an idiot though, and preferred to hide, so I stayed in my room instead.

My eyes have settled down and the swelling has started to retreat. After the past three days, during which I've felt lobotomized, I can now focus and understand what I see, and I don't feel confused any more. But then I went to the bathroom and saw that my face and neck were completely yellow, a deep Moorish saffron yellow, the sort of colour you see painted on the walls of Moroccan houses. I looked like a portrait painted by a small child. The colours and contours of my face had been reinterpreted, a bit like a Picasso painting from his Cubist period. Evidently my bruising had been waiting to surprise me: yesterday I had two black eyes, today I looked jaundiced. But it didn't bother me because I was feeling great and ate everything in the fridge: yogurt, pitta bread and a square of chocolate. It was not enough though and I remained famished, but was too shy to walk into the dining room downstairs and put everyone off their breakfast. 'Enjoy your eggs sunny side up! By the way, do we clash?'

Knowing that Robert will bring me up a *pain au chocolat* I tidied up the room and, hiding in the wardrobe, I got ready to jump out at him when I heard him enter the room. BOO! 'You're better then?' he asked me. 'You look fantastic!' Bless him – he's too short-sighted to notice I'm yellow. I tore the French pastry into small ribbons and poked them into my mouth with a toothbrush.

We always said this was a working holiday, an investment holiday in fact, as it's an investment in the future. Today it felt like a proper holiday for the first time. I was completely at ease with life. We took more photos of my bruises and e-mailed them to our friends. My close friend Melanie Williamson e-mailed back to tell me that she would have liked to have seen the operation, and asked whether that was perverse. Well, she was a medical student before becoming an agent. It sounds like the perfect career path to me.

Later in the day it was off to see the post-operative care assistant again. When Dr Olivier de Frahan saw me he exclaimed, 'What has happened to your face? You are yellow!' For a joke I told him that Robert had beaten me during the night. There was a pause in the conversation. In fact there was no facial reaction, and he simply carried on talking, so I presumed he'd believed me.

Disconcertingly he could not commit to our going home on Monday. We asked if we could see him on Monday morning, but unfortunately he had an American couple scheduled to see him; a man and his wife. He would be operating on the wife at 8 a.m. and the husband six hours later. The couple will be sharing a room at the hospital. The doctor said it worried him that one patient would have to wait throughout the morning to see if their partner was OK. I'd be more worried about them sharing the same room, as going to the toilet for the next twenty-four hours would be like playing blind man's buff!

After the meeting my doctor sent me off to the chemist to get some vitamin K cream for my bruising. The girl in the pharmacy could hardly contain her laughter at the sight of me and it soon became obvious that she was going to have a hernia if she tried to hold in her giggles any more. I felt another one of those Alan Partridge moments coming on again and ran out of the shop. As soon as I got outside I shrieked with laughter. My bruising is so widespread that my sunglasses barely disguise it. I look as though I have been kicked, boxed and strangled simultaneously. Robert hasn't referred to me as the Elephant Man today. Bless his short sight, he thinks I look wonderful and he keeps telling me so.

At my lymphatic-drainage session earlier in the day the care assistant ordered me to stay in the hotel today with only a little walking: 'You must not get tired. Your body is tired. Rest!'

I didn't feel tired, though my brain was still a bit scrambled. Although I wouldn't have attempted to drive in this state, I felt good, and who needs to know their left from right when you're in *gay Paris* anyway. But the hotel room is a little wearing and Robert's DVD collection mainly consists of unappealing macho thrillers. I wanted to go home now.

On the streets of Paris, part of the problem is that I cannot go where there are tourists. I am unrecognizable at the moment, but my voice remains very distinctive. I must be the only person in the world who can phone a call centre in India and get asked 'Is that Toyah Willcox?' as soon as I open my mouth. It's the lisp thing! Among tourists I would stand out as an oddity, especially to children – 'Mummy, why has that woman got a yellow face and a big head?' – and one can always rely on the British to be unsubtle. So museums are out of the question and if I attempt to go up the Eiffel Tower, people might jump off in shock at the sight of me. I will have to be content with sending witty e-mails to inquisitive friends. No doubt as my boredom grows the e-mails will get more daring and vulgar, maybe even faintly obscene. Perhaps a snapshot of myself standing naked in the lift with my bandaged head and a croissant clenched between my buttocks would cheer up a few pals on what might be an otherwise boring Friday night . . .

SATURDAY 28 FEBRUARY 2004

It feels like it's time to go home. I am completely back to normal, both mentally and physically, apart from the fact that the stitches are holding my ears on. What I mean by normal is *my* normal. Once again I have the energy of a five-year-old on orangeade. Having managed six hours' sleep, which is the equivalent of a narcoleptic marathon for me, I woke up with an energy level that needed to be spent. Some people expend this kind of energy by running, pushing weights, shopping or even having copious amounts of sex. In my current situation, however, appearances are deceptive and I still have to keep my blood pressure down or it could burst the dam of my fresh scars, causing them to bleed and bleed.

I decided to alleviate this energy by texting Robert, who was already downstairs having the two-hour breakfast he loves when he is abroad, drinking coffee and reading a heavyweight book. I told him I am lonely. He texted back to say he only had one *pain au chocolat* today so he couldn't bring me one. I replied and told him to have it (so good of me!). I heard nothing back so I texted him again to remind him that I was still lonely. He replied and asked me what he's supposed to do about it. I texted him back with a pitiful 'Pleeeeeeeease'. This did the trick. I could hear someone coming up in the lift and so I hid strategically behind the bedroom door. He opened it and I waited for the tension to build in the silence of our room as he stood trying to figure out where I was, then I made my move. BOO! He exited his skin and looked mightily pissed: 'I thought you needed me! You got me up here just to do that? I hadn't had my two hours at breakfast!'

I reminded him that I could have woken him for a chat at 6 a.m., but instead I waited till 7 a.m. He then produced a squashed *pain au chocolat*, hidden within his *Herald Tribune*, and proceeded to tell me that the staff today were not as good as usual, as they only brought him the one pastry. Calling him a poor old thing I told him lovingly to stick it up his arse. Believe it or not this kind of dialogue creates an atmosphere of calm and congeniality, and we started to talk about the day's news.

My eyes continue to cause me concern. They fluctuate between being OK and then suddenly swollen. Today they are being pulled down by the swelling in the rest of the face, which seemed to have peaked two days ago and hasn't budged since. If I flexed my eye muscles tight I could get them to look as they usually do, and so I told myself to trust the renowned surgeon's choices, and that once the excess water retention in my cheeks disappeared my eyes would revert back to normal. I walked around with my eye muscles flexed.

My doctor wanted me to go to an incredibly trendy hair establishment today and get my hair washed. My scalp was itching and I would love this manky, disinfectant-hardened pile of hair to be washed, especially if it meant that I could go about without my head being wrapped like a mummy. On the downside, the one thing I really didn't want was to sit in a million-dollar hair salon with young, rich and beautiful people all around me swooning at my scars and the metal staples in the backs of my ears and head. I'd rather do the washing myself and let dear old Robert swoon.

In the bathroom with hubby I have been fiddling with my dressings and examining my scars. I pulled the bandage aside to show him that I thought the surgeon had managed to put my ear scar practically in the ear, thus hiding it. Hurray! Robert went pale at the sight of the cut around the ear, and I realized that it's possibly too soon to show him anything.

Looking in the mirror, I quickly noticed that in the space of the last two hours the swelling in my face had reduced dramatically. What a relief! I thought it would take months. The daily massages had obviously paid off.

At 12.15 p.m. we left for the doctor's office for another face massage, followed by a check-up with Dr Olivier de Frahan. The massage was sublime and I fell asleep. The doctor was on good form too, casually dressed in a light-blue, polo-neck, cashmere jumper, which is just the sort of image I would expect for a plastic surgeon. I think he's the rock'n'roll star of the cosmetic-surgery world. Looking at my bruised and yellow face he remarked, 'Good, very good! You heal well, four days and look at you. Out with the stitches under your eye!'

I was overjoyed. Every tiny, neat little step he made with my face was, psychologically, a massive step forward for freedom from bandages, in my view. The scarf-and-glasses routine was wearing thin. I wanted my full hearing back and my full sight. Four days was enough.

The extraction of the stitches under the eye hurt; not a lot, but it took some strength not to scream. The stitches were tight and it was inevitable that the sensitive skin under the lashes was going to be nicked in the cutting of the stitches. It was soon over, and though I was a little 'nicked', it felt great. He had also managed to remove some of the stitches around the ear, which didn't hurt at all. As he did so we had our first real conversation, which was probably because he wasn't under pressure to get to another patient in an operating theatre. I asked him whether he was used to dealing with very beautiful women, and if so, were they demanding and difficult? I don't think he quite understood what I meant, but his reply was fascinating:

'Women come to me who have been beautiful, big, 1980s film stars, and they ask me to help them, make them beautiful again, or at least restore their natural beauty. Youthful. Sometimes their inner light has gone; for different reasons, especially no more love from a man or the public. But if a woman is in love and happy then she is beautiful inside and I can do much more for her.

'I had one woman two years ago, a huge American film star, who came with her agent. She said nothing, but her agent kept saying, "Do you know who this is that you are dealing with? She is a very big star." I explained to him that if she comes to give me her face, it's because she wants *me* to be the star, not her; she is flesh and bone to me. She understood and was fine, very normal and easy to talk to, but the agent? *Phut*! Eventually he went away, and I could get on and do my job with the patient in a normal way.

'The surgeons who are impressed by stars make me frightened because I am not like that. I have a natural relationship with these people, and I understand their worries and the challenges they face. I understand their fears. The way they look is vital to their work. Their career is at stake with the risk they are about to undertake. But ironically their career is also at stake if they *don't* take the risk.

'Cosmetic surgery is a kind of love affair because they give you their face and their image with a lot of trust. You both have to be in the same feeling. It's about mutual trust. It's not only like a love affair, but it also has to be a good one with no divorce, no separation, no heartache and only happiness.'

I knew what he meant when he said it was important for a woman to be loved by a man. I think this is the French way of saying that when a woman is sexually active her skin is radiant. All women know the importance of sex when it comes to rejuvenating skin that has turned dull and grey, because a bit of the old slap and tickle kicks the hormones in. The trouble is that when you're suffering from middle-age spread and you're in your fifties or even sixties, it becomes increasingly difficult to persuade your male friends of the same age (or preferably younger) that they're doing you a service of great medical, physiological and psychological importance. Instead we have to call for the knife!

Twenty minutes later my hair was down – well, it was bandage-free but as hard as a rock, and standing rigidly on end thanks to the solidifying effect of the disinfectant. My doctor had arranged an appointment for me at a celebrity hair salon that accepted his clients, but the thought horrified me and I told him so. I couldn't possibly be seen in a fashionable establishment in my current state, but apparently the doctor sent all his post-operative patients there. I pity the poor thing who had to untangle this mess and try not to touch the line of staples in the back of my head.

As I left he advised me that a lot of my hair will come out while it was being washed, especially the hair that was previously attached to the flesh he'd removed and was too matted to be combed out during the op. The anaesthetic would have caused some hair loss too. I was grateful to him for his honesty once again, but was not surprised to hear the warning as it was a side effect I'd been expecting. My friend Linda Meredith, who had her operation in December, had previously shown me the extent of her hair loss, which had since all grown back.

I protested that I would rather wash my hair myself because I was shy of being seen like this in public, but the doctor insisted that an expert should do the job: 'You will look awful if you try to do this yourself. Besides, everyone is used to seeing this type of thing, everyone has it now.'

The hairdresser's turned out to be a very posh establishment, and far from being kept out of public view, I was placed right in the middle of the salon, completely surrounded by other clients and in full view of the street outside. I felt such a fool. As Robert and I hadn't had any time to have lunch, I'd grabbed a banana on the way, so here I was in a room of exclusively French-speaking fashionable people with a fucking banana in my hand and a hair-do straight from hell. I wanted the floor to open up. While I broke into a cold sweat, and explained that I couldn't bear being on display like this, Jean the manager was delightful in his attempt to reassure me: 'Everyone comes here – we've seen it all before.'

In a mirror I caught a look of horror on the face of the girl who had been assigned the job of washing this lot out, which, because of the bright red disinfectant in my hair and the row of silver staples through my skin, looked far worse than it actually was.

I was ushered over to one of three basins right in front of the rest of the salon; the others were occupied by a bride-to-be and an elderly woman. They must have thought I was roadkill. I looked at them, said 'Sorry!' then sat down, covering my ears with my hands right throughout the wash, not only to protect them, but to hide them from view. The scar tissue around the ear was a bluish colour, deeply bruised, and close up I could have been mistaken for a Victor Frankenstein creation. The washbasins were only inches apart so on either side of me there were women on a nice day out who had ended up having their hair done while sitting next to what looked like a reconstructed blood bath!

Afterwards it felt glorious to be rid of all that matting. Though it had taken quite a while to sort it all out, once my hair had been blow-dried I looked incredible. No one would ever have been able to tell that I had any stitches or staples in my head at all; my hair covered the lot. The staff plucked up the courage to come and have a closer look, and stared at me so intensely that I felt like a new designer outfit on a clothes rail. 'Magnifique work!' was the general consensus, meaning my face, not the blow-dry. I left the place on cloud nine, strutting down the Champs-Elysées like a teenage minx.

I hadn't talked to my manager Jon Roseman all week, so I texted him to say that the operation was a huge success, I was looking a million dollars and I'd written enough words for a week's worth of serialization and a small book. He texted back, 'Great, I suppose a fuck's out of the question?' I replied and told him that 'My ears might fall off.' He responded with, 'You're the best,' and I let him know by return that my husband would willingly 'slip him a crippler' (i.e. engage in buggery, for those unfamiliar with this delightful euphemism). My phone lay silent for the rest of the night.

The manager who oversees all my presenting and advertising (from 'in vision' to 'voiceover'), as well as my corporate work and my writing, is Jon Roseman. I also have an acting agent called Michael Hallett, who controls all my theatre and film work, as well as my dramatic writing (currently at a fledgling stage). The former thinks I had only one choice if I were to continue work as a presenter, and that was to go ahead and have surgery to improve my eyes at the very least; anything else was a bonus. Before I left for Paris I called Jon to check he was confident about what I was doing. Not only did he say that he was certain, but he was also tremendously proud of me because I had the sense to invest in my future. In contrast, however, the latter was very concerned. Michael felt strongly that plastic surgery was not necessary and he wanted me to be moulded by age into becoming a character actress. Previously he had been opposed to my experimenting with Botox, in case it damaged my facial expressions and, as a result, my acting ability, but I was able to prove to him that by having such tiny quantities I was still capable of conveying particular emotions as naturally as before, simply without the lines of anxiety which, until Botox, had been permanently etched on my face.

My argument for surgery is that everyone who is anyone has had something done. I could name some utterly stupendous actresses, character actresses at that, who had facelifts at my age and who have gone on to win Oscars. *And* they still kept a natural look, which is what my surgeon has always intended me to have, and has now succeeded in giving me.

Eventually Michael Hallett came round to see things from my point of view, probably on discovering that most of his highly successful clients had had a nip and a tuck themselves. But one thing Michael definitely didn't want was for the press and the industry to know about it, and part of me agreed. The world I live in thrives on negativity and is almost blind to anything positive. As cynical as that may sound, it's founded upon a very sad truth – we live in a world of resentment. Jon Roseman, on the other hand, wanted to tell the world and was talking about newspaper coverage and publishing deals. I think it's safe to say that Jon was dealing with the short term and that Michael was seeing long term. I was the piggy-in-the-middle, and while I certainly didn't wish to be a martyr to cynicism by outing myself or being outed by others, I also refused to bankrupt myself for the sake of 'high art'. 'Growing old gracefully' is a term that to me means 'fading away quietly', but all I want to do is work, work, work.

SUNDAY 29 FEBRUARY 2004

Waking up after a good night's sleep without having bandages around my head for the first time in six days, my face and neck felt tight as if I was wrapped in cling film. I have heard about this tight sensation from other post-ops, who found it disturbing. However, for me it was exactly the feeling I wanted, as it gave me confidence that my jowls were not touching my chest. I woke in my favourite position, on my left side, which wasn't wise as my ears were still incredibly vulnerable to any pressure or movement. I suffered for it for about an hour by experiencing a slight dizzy sensation.

Since the operation I have been getting raging tinnitus, especially in my right ear. I presumed that this ear was the first to be operated on, and so after it had been cut and the skin repositioned around it, I must then have lain on it for a further two hours while the left ear was being dealt with. As a result I've been hearing a tidal wave in stereo sloshing back and forth through my head, but I remain positive that it will fade away eventually; the operation must have affected the pressure in my ears. I must not forget, therefore, that no matter how well my energy levels have recovered, if I mess with my blood pressure through over-activity or by sleeping on an ear that's completely surrounded by stitches, my body will punish me in return. It will be like this for at least a month and I must acknowledge this.

Today I had a burning ambition to escape from the bedroom. I have been holed up like a bank robber, or a subversive who's changed her identity, for a week, and consequently I've developed a strong will and the courage to go out and embrace life to the full. The carpet in this bedroom has begun to suffer under my pacing feet and I've exhausted all the hiding places from where I can jump out and scare the wits out of my husband. I needed some sunlight on my skin as I had started to feel like a vampire banished from daylight.

The feelings of utter joy, confidence and relief are almost beyond description and it is a combination of positive sentiments that grows stronger daily. I have done the right thing and chosen the right person with whom to do it, whose skills have proved invaluable.

I went down to breakfast for the first time since I arrived at the hotel, and part of me felt as though I'd joined some exclusive club, an expensive, classy elite. Other people achieve this by becoming members of the best golf clubs in the world, some by purchasing the best cars. There will be some who probably feel this way just by shopping at Chanel or Versace, but for me, clothes have never had the effect of making my tiny frame feel superior as I've never grown beyond the size of an average child. Instead this surgery has made me grow in stature, and rather than feel ashamed that vanity has driven me to make the biggest mistake of my life, I feel I have stepped out of the cage of predictable ageist entrapments.

At breakfast I ate a meal, my first in a week. After losing some valuable weight over the last few days I needed to start building myself up again because my body needed vital nutrients. Today I felt so hungry that I was determined to eat well. My jaw was still a little stiff from being clamped open for four hours and I had to push food into my mouth, but it was getting more flexible by the hour. In fact my whole recovery was evolving with every minute that passed by.

All around me in the dining room were super-posh people in suits or sportswear. I decided that the people in the suits were weekenders who were as impressed as I was by this grand hotel, and those in the jogging kits were the true billionaires. Robert and I started a guessing game in which we pondered, 'Who's here for surgery and who's just had it?' One had to remember that today was Sunday, and so all surgery would commence tomorrow, which meant that everyone was eating with relative calm rather than stuffing their faces in anticipation of it being their 'last meal'.

There was one couple sitting two tables away, a man and a woman, who from their conversation sounded Dutch. The man was in his fifties with long hair and may as well have had a neon sign above his head saying 'rock musician', alongside one above his female companion's head that said 'rock musician's wife'. Both Robert and I agreed that they were in for joint surgery tomorrow, which prompted the following question from Robert: 'Wife, do I need a facelift?' I told him not to be so absurd; no man needs a facelift – it's the exclusive domain of women. Then I spent the rest of breakfast wondering what had made me say that. Was it male programming that had rubbed off on me after years working in a sexist industry or was I being sexist against men? Did I truly believe that men never suffered from the personal disappointment caused by ageing that we women feel? Or was it simply because I knew he'd make a rotten patient in recovery? Either way I didn't want him to have surgery because I loved him how he was; in fact I'd never fancied him more.

I could now look at the scars around my ear and the staples at the back of my head without flinching. I imagined that the staples – a three-inch row of silver-coloured, larger-than-office-stationery staples – on each side of my head would be there for quite a few weeks. My greatest fear was that the main visible scar would be the one at the front of the ear, but rather brilliantly the doctor had run it over the small frontal bone of the ear and deep into the crevice of the ear lobe. After two weeks it will be hard to trace; after a further four months it will be invisible.

Luckily I have the thickest hair in the world and I am confident it will grow back over the scarring at the back of the head as thick as it ever was to obscure the path of the scalpel. This cut is the most fascinating. I would never have guessed in a thousand years the trajectory the scalpel had taken to create something that looked and felt like the neck of a ten-year-old. The doctor had cut close to the ear lobe and around the deep recess at the back of the ear and out into the shaved lower hair line, dipping down like a musical clef, at the point at which the hair grows closest to the back of the ear, thus making it almost impossible to detect. It is as if the eye of the surgeon is like that of a dressmaker; it is artistry as much as practical skill, and it doesn't upset or repulse me, but instead it draws me in. When people all have such contrasting face shapes, skull sizes and skin types, how did any human being reach the conclusion that this was the right cut to make? What sort of practice did they have? Was it on friends and family, like a hairdresser? If not friends or family, then on whom did they practice? Surely not corpses? However the technique evolved, I was deeply bloody impressed.

Robert and I walked to the Arc de Triomphe today. It was a cold day and I was well wrapped in a gold scarf and also wearing sunglasses. People kept looking at me, presumably because I had the air of someone who didn't want to be recognized. I imagined that my quest for privacy had made them more inquisitive, but Robert pointed out it was because I looked incredibly glamorous.

We've been blissfully holed up in a hotel room for seven days, and it's been possibly one of the most romantic times of my life. I've laughed more this week than I can ever remember, and we've both loved the exclusivity of each other's company. Out on the streets of Paris, though, we were surrounded by people and I felt a bit freaked. We stopped for lunch, then walked a little more and took a break for some ice cream, my major vice. Despite the fact that it was a chilly wintry day, I sampled six different flavours: pistachio, coffee, vanilla, chocolate, melon and toffee. It wasn't long before I discovered why the nurse had discouraged me from eating ice cream when I first came round from the operation: first my facial muscles went stiff, then began to spasm, before starting to feel rock solid. Walking back to the hotel we also had a few hills to ascend and although we did this slowly, I couldn't help feeling that I was tempting fate, particularly as the doctor was always warning me against climbing up hills. We had been out walking for about three hours in some rather cold temperatures, and by the time we reached our hotel room my face had started to swell again. Damn! This morning I looked fantastic and now I'd set myself back a few days. The doctor won't be impressed.

At only 6 p.m. we settled into bed for the night, as today had been a long day for me. We didn't go to sleep immediately, however, and an hour later, while reading a newspaper, I noticed that my neck and ears were feeling tight. I didn't feel ill or different in any way other than this tightness; there was no burning sensation or any accompanying pain. As I wasn't concerned enough to go and check on myself in the mirror, I carried on reading my paper.

Just after 7 p.m. I had a phone call from Dr Olivier de Frahan. Although it was his day off, he was ringing to check that all was OK and to find out whether I was happy with my hair after Saturday's visit to the hairdresser. He was deeply apologetic about the hair he had had to shave off in order to cut around the ear and issued another honest reminder about possible hair loss after the anaesthetic. It struck me that he was able to show a deep understanding of the underlying fears women have; perhaps he was simply more sensitive than most to other people's needs. Anyway as far as I was concerned there were no problems. If anything my hair looked even better after a little thinning out, as it's so thick and always looked like a mop. I suggested to the doctor rather bossily that he deserved a day off, so he should leave me be and get some rest himself.

Then I went into the bathroom and caught sight of myself. This morning much of the swelling had gone down, and I'd looked bloody stunning, but now my head appeared wider somehow. It seemed that the scar tissue around my ears had swelled, which it had never done before, with the effect that it was pulling my eyes out and downwards. I checked the colouration around my ears. It was a little blue, but there was no redness and only a little heat. I didn't know what to do.

After asking Robert to switch on the computer and open up the pictures he had taken of me that morning, I studied them carefully, and could see that my eye shape was being distorted by swelling, but only slightly. Robert couldn't quite notice it, and just commented that he thought there was something different about me. The left side of my face – the side that had been almost normal – was more swollen than the right, and on both sides there was swelling around the ear. I didn't know what to do about this, and wondered whether I should speak to the doctor again. I'd heard from other people who'd had facelifts that if they got hot or stressed they could experience an uncomfortable tightness, which would make sense of what was happening to me. Perhaps we'd walked in the cold air for too long. I was solely to blame for that, so I decided not to bother the doctor on his day off.

I wrapped my ears with lint tucked behind to protect the scars and went to bed a little tense, while doing my best to try to visualize the swelling dissipating. But every negative thought was entering my head. What if I have the hospital 'superbug', MRSA? What if there is internal bleeding? I just hoped and prayed that all was well and that the slight swelling was natural.

MONDAY 1 MARCH 2004

The swelling hadn't increased in the night, but neither had it decreased. Today the doctor was in surgery from 8 a.m. until 2.30 p.m., and I was due to see him before his next operation at 3 p.m. I felt bad about that; the poor man probably wouldn't have chance to eat because I'd asked to see him to get the all-clear before leaving for England with Robert this evening. I decided that I'd need to have a plan B on standby in case the doctor insisted I stayed in Paris for a while longer. I feel well enough to cope alone; the confusion I've been suffering is subsiding, though I still can't tell my left from my right, which isn't ideal when crossing the road in another country. But I do feel capable of surviving on my own. My main worry is that I don't want to get home and have my face drop off!

One positive effect caused by the swelling was that it had subtly infiltrated the fibres of my nose and smoothed the lines of my skin, which enabled me to recall how I looked in my younger days; because we generally have thicker skin when we're young, the nose is more fleshy and rounded, which is how my nose seemed now. No camera can pick up what you truly see in a mirror, and nor can it catch the truth of the effects of age the way your own eyes do, which is why it's very difficult to remember exactly how you looked twenty years ago. The picture is erased from our memory; even old photographs can only catch a percentage of who we once were. I didn't remember what it was like to look in the mirror and never question if this or that crease could be dealt with, but today, thanks to the presence of this uncomfortable swelling, I could actually recollect how I used to be and I found myself caught up in a wave of nostalgia.

So many memories kept flooding back: the first time I was the object of someone's attention; the feeling of confident flirtation; how young men naturally moved when attracted to someone; how their hips seemed to take on a life of their own and betrayed the fact that a kiss on the cheek meant far more than friendship; the light in the eyes when everyday life was about seeking discreet tactility; how crushes fuelled your ambitions and pushed you into doing things you would otherwise never attempt, all in the name of showing off the peacock's tail; and the wonderful way men used to push themselves tight into your groin unconsciously, and how it so simply and uncontrollably ignited every ambition and aim in life.

My God! My life is so different now. I have learned to live without flirtation and attention, and I don't think this facelift will change that, even though some women do this because they believe it will make them sexier. I need a lot more than a 'subtle' facelift to trick the opposite sex into thinking that I am ripe for picking. I need a body lift! But it is fabulous to remember that that is how it used to be.

Robert and I went to the doctor's office for the last time. All our cases were packed and we were ready for a fast getaway to the train station. In the waiting room was a little, wrinkled old lady. I guessed that she was in her late seventies and she must have had her eyes done as there were plasters under her bottom lids. Brave broad! She too was in that Parisian uniform of the brown fur coat, teetering high heels and eyelashes covered in spidery mascara.

Dr Olivier de Frahan arrived dressed in full operating-theatre gown; even his shoes had bags over them. I felt awful – he'd given up his lunch hour to see me. He checked me over carefully, but wasn't unduly concerned about my swelling, which was a relief. I was given strict instructions on how to maintain the scabs – I had to clean them with surgical spirit – and was told to rest and eat well. I squeezed his hand and thanked him. He had been quite stunning.

Robert and I made it in time for the 4 p.m. train. The customs officer couldn't quite look me in the eye, for it must have seemed as though the lovely, quiet, bespectacled man at my side, Robert, had given me a good beating. Once we were settled on the train the staff also looked a little too long at my face, but I was playing the 'I've been skiing and had an accident with a tree' game. My eyes looked like those of a panda, and my skin was as yellow as a banana. One of my biggest fears was of being identified, but my face was still swollen out of all recognition, without looking freaky. I actually looked about fifteen years younger because my face was so round, and my hair colour was radically different too.

On arrival in London, we jumped into a taxi. We had already decided that I would not talk in the cab as the lisp always gives me away. We stepped through the doors of our London home, and a vast sense of relief swam through my veins. I've done it and not been discovered! At 8 p.m. I crashed into bed exhausted.

I'm due to stay here alone for the rest of the week while Robert returns to Nashville, his base in the USA. He'll be coming back to London in ten days' time, and then we'll go to our main home in Worcestershire. Once there I'll be able to enjoy some much-needed peace and quiet, even though privacy is far easier to find in London than anywhere else in the country as nobody is in the least bit interested in your comings and goings. The doctor will be in London on Friday and he can satisfy us both that all is AOK.

TUESDAY 2 MARCH 2004

I woke at about 1 a.m. thinking about why I seem to have suddenly developed premature Alzheimer's. I have lost my ability to spell even the simplest of words and I cannot even comprehend basic technical things such as entering a password into the computer. Before leaving for the US Robert had discreetly mentioned that after a full week of my being post-operative, he was somewhat concerned about the state of my mental faculties. The anaesthetic should have worn off and so there shouldn't have been any lingering symptoms other than tiredness.

I wondered if it had anything to do with the fact that eleven days ago I stopped taking all my usual supplements in case they were putting undue stress on my liver and kidneys. It was one of the many safety measures I took to ensure a quick recovery. I stopped all my herbal detox pills, including acidophilus for the intestines, hemp seed oil, cod liver oil and vitamin E, especially as the latter can raise blood pressure, which is the last thing I'd need during or after my surgery.

But Robert was right. I'm not *compos mentis*, I'm '*thickus dullius*', and there has to be a reason for it. So today I decided to begin taking all the supplements that my body had grown used to and I'd add a vitamin tonic too – Metatone from Boots, a product for convalescing that I've used as a dressing-room tonic for years, particularly when I wasn't able to eat enough food because of tight costumes or if I was about to spend the next two hours running around like a banshee. I'm hopeful that this should kick-start my energy levels. Let's see what happens and how I feel tomorrow.

Yesterday's travelling really took it out of me and to top everything off Robert left for Nashville this morning at half past seven. Though he will only be gone for ten days, after nineteen years of marriage it still tugs at my heartstrings whenever he leaves. The timing isn't great so soon after my treatment, but if he doesn't go he will resent me in the end; he is used to his freedom and, after all, I'm over the worst of my personal journey.

I was toying with the idea of driving to our main home in the Midlands alone last night, but I was too exhausted. Instead I ended up staying in London and having an early night with Robert. This morning I still felt as though I shouldn't waste my precious energy on driving, especially as I'd be seeing the doctor for a check-up on Friday at Claridge's. So after Robert left for the airport I tried to get back into my old routine, but dragging my legs somewhat. I really had no energy but I was determined to be as active as I was before the operation.

I changed the bedding, which took me two hours. Overnight my body seems to have gained about twenty stone in weight. I tried to write but I couldn't concentrate properly and I ended up staring in the mirror studying my scars. Luckily, because the mirrors in my bathroom are on three sides, I could get a really good look with the aid of a hand mirror. As scars go, especially this type comprising deeply rearranged skin, they looked bloody good. There wasn't even that much of a scab there, which was just as well because when I left the doctor yesterday, he told me: 'Don't pick the crust, only *I* do that!' I think he cleaned most of it off daily, and though there was a little scab around the stitches, I wasn't compelled to start pulling at it.

I've been finding it increasingly hard to sleep on my back and have been waking up totally relaxed on my left ear, which is still numb from the operation. Then I remember that 50 per cent of my scar is around that ear and I jump up in shock. So the 'crusts' are probably working themselves off in my sleep. No doubt I will get a telling-off on Friday.

Today I noticed for the first time how painful the staples looked in the hairline. If it weren't for the fact that my neck was like a baby's, this sight would probably have made me scream. I looked like a cross between Frankenstein's monster and a Sunday roast, and because I can't see the staples without the aid of a mirror, if I hadn't seen them close up I'm certain I would have gone food shopping with my hair up, oblivious to the fact that I was displaying them to my fellow shoppers. One thing is evident: the doctor has made sure no one will see a thing once I am healed and my hair has grown back. The scar by my ear goes just into the ear and the rest is so tight to the lobe and the back of the ear that it's invisible even now. In fact the only tell-tale sign is where the scar cuts across horizontally into the hairline; even then it's where the ear is at its greatest width. Someone would have to pin me down and pull the ear back to see it properly. I am a frank person and when it comes to future photo sessions I will be certain to tell the hair stylists, and just hope they comply when I ask them to keep their mouths shut!

The only practical problem I can envisage concerning my scars is if I get a role that requires my head to be shaved. I can't really see that happening, however, and if it does it's probably likely that any woman of my age will have had a facelift, therefore I'll be able to save the make-up person the time and expense of adding painted-on scars to the hairline.

There is one part of the surgery that I find distressing and I think it will take the longest to heal. The area around the front bit of my ear is the part that has suffered the most trauma and reconstruction, and as the skin is translucent (well, it is to me), I can see this deep, dark, angry blue beneath the surface, especially by my left ear which has become more swollen than the right. It's subtle. It's not a bruise. It's where the skin has been pulled away in order to reconstruct muscle. In fact it could even be muscle that I am seeing. But where everything else on my face could pass for normal, I am aware that this is a deep trauma cut for the body to deal with and it will take time to get back to its former state. This is the only scar that gives me the creeps. It is not human to me, but purely anatomical.

My last attempt at trying to have an ordinary day was to walk half a mile to Sainsbury's to get fruit and surgical spirit. I'd like to say the fruit was for my scars and the spirit for consumption, but sadly it was the other way round. I walked a little like a zombie, but that wasn't too out of place in Chiswick at 7 o'clock on a Tuesday evening. Immediately I noticed a change in how people were reacting to me. As someone who prefers not to dress flashily I'm pretty good at blending in, but the change in my social status within the crowd had altered dramatically already. Before I went to Paris, men of any age would subconsciously become impatient with me if I got in their way. Now, apart from not being recognized at all, which is unusual in itself, I was being noticed in a positive way. There were smiles on offer. The irritation I used to sense from people had gone. My operation had tricked these people into accepting me as something I am not – younger. It's a different world! Eight days after the operation, the invisibility curse with which I was afflicted has gone. I now have a place in the crowd again; the 'tired, irritable hag' that was wrongly imagined by others has disappeared. I will never let her return if I can help it, as being judged falsely by others is sometimes not unlike living a prison sentence.

The doctor had asked me to clean certain areas around the ear with surgical spirit every day, which struck me as an odd request because as a musician I used spirit to harden my fingertips for guitar playing to desensitize them. I would hate to 'harden' any skin on my face, but I followed the doctor's instructions, as I only needed to apply it until Friday.

I went to bed early.

WEDNESDAY 3 MARCH 2004

Good! Good! And bloody good! The ga-ga effect is wearing off. It was definitely the combination of post-operative body shock and my having stopped taking supplements. For example, for the last eight days I've had the energy and IQ of a zombie, and when I was writing my journal in the mornings I had to ask Robert to repeat the spellings of virtually every word containing more than five letters. After a perfect night's sleep, however, this morning I was up and writing at 7 a.m., and the thoughts were flowing.

It took the whole of yesterday to recover from the journey back on Monday. The intensity of having to act normal for the whole day had worn me out. Well, I couldn't travel on Eurostar as a middle-aged woman who was feeling brittle from her first facelift and had allowed the floodgate of emotions to open for all to see. Heaven forbid the shame of it if I'd reclined in the train seat and wailed about the unfairness of life. Not that I felt that way, of course, but I was dreading Robert's absence over the next few days. I do feel some embarrassment at the fact my vanity has got the better of me, though, as I'm not quite strong enough to sit out the onslaught of wrinkles for the next thirty years in the name of feminism. Why the hell should I when there are people

like Dr Olivier de Frahan in the world? I'm starting to
suspect that many of the so-called 'naturally beautiful'
older actresses I see on the television may have possibly
had a little bit of help at some point in their lives.
Anyway, I was up and writing, and that's all I cared
about.

Another precious insight that occurred to me this
morning was how mind-numbingly dull daytime TV can
be. It has only dawned on me, after ten years of having it
on to provide mere 'background' noise, that it is
incredibly negative about 'normality'. In fact it is either
insultingly patronizing or morbidly fatalistic. But
generally I do love television. To me it's the greatest
learning medium since the invention of the printing press,
so why can't the powers-that-be realize that its audiences
all want one prime thing in life – to achieve a better life,
not to listen to others talking down to them. I always
have it on and fall into a trance, but in Paris of course I
escaped it, perhaps even missed it. Once away from it,
though, I was free of all the false ideals it projects about
the perfect family, how much this dress costs, how you
can win a holiday or a car. In Paris it didn't take long for
my mind to be liberated from that humdrum world, and
instead thoughts of how to live the perfect, most active
and rebellious old age started to take shape.

This morning the telly is OFF.

It seems that by putting the Omega 3 and Omega 6
back in my diet, my brain has kicked into gear. I had
experienced this twice before in the last year; both
occasions when I had been forced to come off the
supplements. The first time was on *I'm A Celebrity, Get
Me Out Of Here!* in April and May 2003. The
contestants were not allowed to take anything into the
jungle other than the clothes on their backs and any life-
sustaining medication. As supplements were not
considered life-sustaining I had to embark on the
adventure without any. Ironically the production team felt

that cigarettes and alcohol were vital to the well-being of the individual, so the non-smokers among us were treated to the smell of tobacco in the heart of the Australian rainforest.

It didn't occur to me that surviving without my supplements would be a problem. I thought that my skin would suffer, but I could live with that. Thanks to the wonder of hindsight, however, a massive question has been answered for me.

Within two days of being in the jungle I became quite ill. The symptoms suggested I was experiencing accelerated diabetes, and the on-site doctor couldn't fathom why. He knew dehydration was a part of it, along with the shock of a sudden diet change, but there was still a dramatic decline in health as far as he was concerned and he kept a close eye on me daily. On about my fourth day in the jungle he called me to the medical hut for blood tests. Firstly he couldn't get any blood out of me, which was a key sign of dehydration, and secondly when he tested me for diabetes, my blood sugar levels were incredibly high. It was a relief to find that I hadn't developed diabetes, but he had definite proof that I was experiencing difficulties, and so after that he'd sneak me biscuits to eat if I felt I was going to pass out, but only two per day. Other than that we had a limited amount of rice and soya beans to eat each day to give us the calorific equivalent of a thousand calories a day.

It later transpired that, owing to a miscalculation by the production team, for the first four days we had only been on about five hundred calories a day, while still having to be active in collecting wood, taking part in tasks and fending off the bugs on just half the necessary rations. As far as the doctor was concerned this still didn't explain my illness, and while watching us all on camera at least ten hours a day to make sure we were avoiding the hazards of spiders and snakes, he was also checking that I was looking after myself.

From what he could see I was doing everything right: drinking five litres of water a day, pacing myself and trying to eat handfuls of soya beans regularly. I was already used to these types of conditions, as for countless days and weeks during my working life I have survived on five hundred calories a day, even while starring in West End productions, simply to keep my weight down. But I had never been ill like this before. By the third day in the jungle I could hardly move and my vision was being obscured by white clouds (the first stage of diabetes). I could cope with this as I was tough enough to fight through these kinds of physical barriers – believe me, I'm fucking strong – but the one thing I couldn't fight was the appalling fact that my brain was apparently dead to thought and imagination. It was like I'd been reduced to a monosyllabic celebrity twerp. Never mind physically pushing myself through a pain barrier, by day four, words had begun to fail me and the on-site doctor couldn't do any more to help: it was, er . . . a mystery.

Now I understood that it was the lack of essential daily supplements that had caused the problem, so the cure would have been so simple had I known.

For a number of years, my diet has been geared towards optimum nutritional absorption, and focused on achieving good health throughout menopause and in old age. Five years ago I cut down on all dairy, wheat, meat and processed foods to the point where I don't stock them in any of my homes. I therefore try to avoid unnecessary excess carbohydrates, fats or refined sugars. So my diet consists of soya, fruit (mainly blueberries every day), oats, vegetables (including fresh carrot juice and ginger twice weekly), nuts, pulses, and of course a high amount of oil supplements. Also I wouldn't dream of touching anything containing hydrogenated vegetable oil, which as far as I am concerned carries a death sentence and is the primary cause of the obesity epidemic we are experiencing throughout the western world. The stuff is like concrete, completely indigestible, and fortunately, out in the jungle, I was hundreds of miles away from it.

Nutrition is one of the key interests I have in life. It is a brilliant science that never ceases to amaze, and every aspect of it fascinates me. In the past few years, during which time I have realized that we literally are what we eat, I observed my body's responses to certain foods, and have been keeping a food diary along the way. We are all different in our good and bad responses to diet, as it's a purely individual matter, but over a period of about four years I discovered that my body's main enemies were refined sugars and carbohydrates, red meat and certain fruits (for example, mango causes me joint pains). As a consequence I was able to come up with a diet that suited my body, which resulted in a clearer head, less body fat, and no aches and pains. Now I truly believe that we can cure minor ills through knowing what our bodies need nutritionally.

In the jungle the simple loss to my diet of the natural sugar content in fruit, and also the high oil content in fish oils, meant that not only was my body experiencing shock but that my brain was also being starved. I could still function at the lowest possible energy level, but think and be creative? Not a chance.

The second time I experienced these effects was in November 2003. I'd started a two-year course designed to help improve my dyslexia, having been diagnosed with not only that but also with dyspraxia. The course is called the Dore Programme, which I had first encountered while shooting a short film about how it has accelerated the learning skills in children and adults.

Despite having always known I was dyslexic, I had never associated the condition with being a cause of the permanent frustrations I experienced when trying to communicate an idea. During the filming of this project I asked to be tested and the results proved that my dyspraxia had got worse as I grew older. Soon after I started the course, which is designed around balance exercises, there was an improvement, but not without a number of side effects, such as becoming grumpy for short periods of time and losing my sense of distance from various objects.

The treatment is fabulously simple, perhaps deceptively so, but it works. In someone with dyslexia the brain's neurones are dysfunctional and the cerebellum needs activating; the nerve system at the stem of the brain needs to be encouraged to grow or make contact with the frontal lobe. On this course you are given a series of balance and memory exercises to reawaken the cerebellum to enable it to start communicating with the frontal lobe. Though it may sound technical, it is actually simple and effective, but in order for the course to work completely, all the things that have allowed your brain to trick you into thinking it is working properly have to be taken away. For that is how the dyslexic brain works – it dupes its owner and the outside world into believing that everything is normal and functioning well. My 'helpers' are Omega 3 and Omega 6 oils, which have been scientifically proven to make the brain more efficient, but in the case of a dyslexic they help you bypass what should be normal cerebellar development. This doesn't mean that supplements can impair development, far from it, in fact; just that they help dyslexics to find other neurone routes.

So in November 2003, I reluctantly stopped all supplements in order to make the course fully effective. By December I couldn't remember the lines for my play and my driving skills had begun to waver. I'd temporarily lost my peripheral senses and, as a result, with me becoming increasingly more confused at the wheel, my poor car was forever being reversed into walls and bollards. When I called the dyslexia centre I was told that I had to go through this barrier in order for the cerebellum to kick in, and it would all be worthwhile. In response my argument was that I was about to embark on ninety-six shows in the next six weeks for which I couldn't remember any lines, and as for my driving, I wasn't safe. So we agreed that I could start taking Omega 3 again, but not Omega 6, simply because they were so efficient in helping the brain work that there would have been no point in continuing with the course. To cut a long story into a single sentence, I went back on my oils and within twenty-four hours I was back to normal. In the jungle without these supplements, therefore, I believe the same reaction occurred, and again after my surgery in February. I went la-la.

And the moral of this story? I think that all fish oils should be available to everyone for free. And in the jungle? I remained as sick as a dog until I got out and consumed fresh fruit and vegetables and tons of fish oils!

At 2 p.m. I couldn't resist the temptation to touch my head, twitch some stitches, tap my scabs and scratch some staples. It felt . . . well, nice! Bloody nice, in fact; especially the staples, which were pain-free, yet itchy. Basically I was fiddling. It was as if I wanted it all over with in that instant so I could get on with my life. I'd had ten days of it and now I wanted to be normal. So I found myself in front of the mirror with ears that hadn't seen water in nearly two weeks and I cleaned the insides with cotton buds and surgical spirit. The doctor wouldn't be amused, but he might understand my feelings. The 'guck' I got out – old blood and plugs of wax – was surely better out than in, in this case? Well, what's done is done now, but what I really wanted to do was to finish it off with a hot flannel wash of the whole area, but even I knew that it wouldn't be wise; infection was still a possibility, and had to be avoided at all costs.

Time heals. This could not be more true. Patience allows time to do its work. But patience? I have none!

To distract myself I decided to turn the TV on in the name of convalescence, and saw an actress friend of mine on an afternoon show. She's forty-five years old, the same age as me, a brilliant and successful actress of stage, TV and film, and the first thing I noticed was her neck. I hated myself for it because I was doing to her what I have accused other people of unfairly doing to me. Though she is stunning, intelligent and talented, I was focusing on her one weak feature – her neck. What is this? Some animal instinct to criticize others, especially women?

Perhaps this is a burden that only women have to carry, because I am not aware I do this to men, unless they've developed a pot belly overnight. Men to me are more attractive in their forties, fifties, and even sixties. Why do we judge women by their faces and necks? No matter how beautiful you are – and it is possible to be beautiful with age, as she is – there is no doubt that the condition of the neck can distract from the beauty of the face and here was the case proven. Men are positively squeamish about such things and it appears that so am I. A hanging neck, wrinkled hands, and that true indicator of time, 'cellulite', all seem to disempower women. We could live with it, but it's the opposite sex who constantly remind us, without hesitation and with little self-consciousness, that they cannot bear it, by rendering us invisible once we hit forty. It makes me hanker for that period in the history of mankind when fertility sculptures celebrated large curvy women with robust, sensual thighs. Did this ideal of beauty mean women had to work hard at being fat? Now that is something I could fantasize over: a life condemned to eating – yes, please.

I felt smug. My neck was 'scraggy' ten days ago and it wasn't till now that I realized that the looseness of the neck through age could add years to a beautiful face. I almost phoned my acting agent to tell him to watch the programme because the lady in question had just been Botoxed; I could tell by the smoothness of her skin and the raised eyebrows. Only another 'Botoxee' would know this, of course, but it proved to me that if your neck gave your age away then the smoothing power of the Botox did nothing but emphasize flaws in other areas. The trick is to sort out both problem areas with the tightening of the neck and intelligent use of Botox, as each complements the other.

What about the rest of the body? I don't yet know the tricks for arms and hands, but I will be keeping my ear to the ground. You only hear about the good guys through rumour and hearsay, as no one in the business voluntarily surrenders information about whom to go to or what to take to remedy the effects of age on your body. The megastars who have found the elixir of youth that prolongs their mystery, interest and careers are certainly not going to shout it from the rooftops so that everyone else can book appointments with their precious physicians.

The search to find the next thing to lessen the signs of age is now a part of my life. It's not an obsession, but is simply a way of life, fuelled by the desire to discover that something can be done. Being aware that there is always something out there that can help make a small improvement has a massive effect; for example, the young can wear concealer under their eyes after a late night. I believe that in time the old will have simpler and more accessible ways of disguising their years, but personal research should continue to play an important part, otherwise you could end up with a high-street product that has made it to the front of the counter simply as a result of being owned by a cosmetics firm with a billion-pound advertising budget. This world is about money, but not necessarily about the best product for the problem. You have to find out about other people's surgery, and consumers need to open up and reveal what has worked for them. Silence in these cases is a crime, and is responsible for every bad facelift and every cosmetic mistake a woman or man has had to endure.

In the last few months I haven't had any sex drive, which is odd for me. No sex drive equals no ambition, I have always thought. Both have deserted me for about three months, and that's the scariest sign of age, surely? I enjoy both these aspects of myself and I don't want to be free of them for a long time yet. No more sleepless nights lusting after Brad Pitt, and no more early mornings hunting for that job you really want? Never! I put it down to anxiety over the operation, which had been on my mind 24/7. Even going onstage over Christmas 2003 I would find myself mid-song thinking, 'What if I go and bugger all this up?' But as of today my libido is back with a vengeance and my hubby is 2,000 miles away. Damn! Here I am with a high sex drive, a black eye, a swollen face and staples in the back of my head. Anyone for a dance?

At 4.30 p.m., my mobile rang – it was my father. 'How are you? I haven't talked to you for a while. How was your holiday?' he asked, knowing something was up because for the last week only Robert had talked to him. Not only is he a wily old fox who could get blood from a stone, but he is also one of the few who have supported me through thick and thin, and I decided I could not lie any more.

'Dad, it wasn't a holiday. I've had an operation,' I confessed.

'I knew it! It's your eyes – you've had them done, haven't you?' was his surprising response.

'I've had a facelift,' I admitted. 'It's a huge success and I cannot tell you how brilliant Robert has been.'

'I guessed it! I've left a message on the kitchen table at your house telling you so. I'm really pleased. You had to get it done – you were looking awful! Could the surgeon do anything for me?'

Can you believe it? Even an eighty-three-year-old man thinks I've done the right thing. It's starting to make me wonder, though. I didn't think I looked *that* bad before. Is the ageing process the new leprosy?

THURSDAY 4 MARCH 2004

Last night at around 7.30 p.m. I hit a milestone. My energy went skywards. I wasn't going to abuse how good I suddenly felt in case I went and blew it, but I felt completely up to speed both mentally and physically. Popping out to get food I felt I could have embarked on one of my two-hour eight-mile walks, but common sense prevented me.

At about 6 p.m. yesterday, a time when calm usually descends as all the agents and managers begin heading off to the theatre or dinner, the phone went crazy, and half an hour later all my work plans for 2004 had changed: instead of touring in a musical I was going to be touring in a rock band. This sort of thing is a common occurrence in my life and I like the possibility of sudden change very much. It drives everyone else around me crazy though, from the poor guy who runs my website to costume-makers who have their deadlines shortened, but we all cope. I am not chained to anything or anyone and for a good yearly income I have incredible freedom.

So the tour of a musical I expected to start in August 2004 has moved to spring 2005, and in its place I would be doing a rock tour with Nick Heyward, which to me sounds like twenty-four-hour party time. My one-woman show, a concept I came up with in October 2003, has got the go-ahead to go into workshop stage for September this year and into the theatres in summer 2005. This gives me a kick up the backside as it doesn't even have a title yet, but to me it is the icing on the cake, as I want this to be the year that I write my way into the next phase of my life. In fact the year is looking perfect. I have plenty of time to recover and write.

While clearing up a pile of paperwork last night, I discovered a five-year plan that I'd written in 2000. This was not a good year for me, after all the build-up to the new millennium, and all the talk of new beginnings and new opportunities. In fact the year had been a frustrating anti-climax; it felt as if my life was constipated. Being the eternal optimist back then as I am now, I thought it wise to start deciding exactly what it was that I wanted from life. Surprisingly I didn't really know. Commitment to any one thing was hard and vague, and what came out on paper surprised me, as it had never before occurred to me that not only do I have materialistic priorities, but I am still insecure about the stability of everything in my life. Ever since 2000, therefore, I've been writing an annual 'wish list' as an exercise and a reminder to myself what it is exactly I am hoping to achieve. Then, every so often, I rediscover these hidden pieces of paper and reading them either gives me a laugh or a jolt.

The 2000 list was a sort of wish list in which I committed myself to my dreams. The reason for it is that some people believe that by writing down dreams, ambitions and intentions they can come true, because in a way you are sowing a seed into your consciousness, which enables even the smallest intention to take root. I must have read about this in *The Artist's Way* or one of the many popular self-help books that have been around for decades. They are fantastic for dressing-room reading, and are brilliant when your life begins to suffer from constipation.

The year 2000 list was as follows:

FIVE-YEAR PLAN

1. I will earn enough to pay off the mortgage on my cottage and have major renovations carried out [I had just bought a new property]: £140,000.
2. I will earn enough to have two good holidays a year: £5,000.
3. I will earn enough to have necessary plastic surgery: £20,000.
4. I will evolve and work continually towards becoming a name actress, writer and presenter.

5. I will keep my contacts growing.
6. I will establish strong working bonds with directors, writers and producers.
7. I will write, produce and tour a new album.
8. I will produce my first novel.
9. I will live life to the full.

By March 2004 I'd achieved all of these except number 2. I cannot get my head around taking holidays! They bore me shitless. Obviously numbers 4 to 9 are ongoing life commitments, but all the talk about money was quite a shock. By my age money shouldn't be on the agenda. It appears the more I earn, the more I want! Shouldn't the 'new youth' of the 'new millennium' be like those adventure-seeking Edwardians one hundred years ago, going off on year-long safaris to wild and inhospitable places like Las Vegas? That apart, I firmly believe that if you don't know what you want from life then the universe cannot conspire to help you, so I'm still trying to establish my priorities year by year.

Yesterday afternoon I was looking in the mirror, thoroughly inspecting my eleven grand's worth of surgery, and estimating that I must have paid about £300 per stitch, when I noticed that there was a small pea-sized lump just under the scar of my left eye. Had an internal stitch slipped? Was it my fault? Had I been too active? 'Oh, bugger!' I thought.

It was hard, it didn't hurt, and it didn't move with my eye muscles when I flexed them, which I often do at the moment, in the hope of getting the swelling to reduce. Perhaps it was an irritated nerve, something that has gone into spasm or shock, and it would eventually disappear. The only thing that concerns me is that I don't want to have to go back to Paris for any extra corrections. I'm ready to get on with my life here, especially as the future is shaping up far better than I could have hoped.

At 7 p.m. this evening I walked over to my manager's house for supper. Jon Roseman and his partner, Danielle, wanted to see all the gory bits first. Jon has been a huge supporter of this surgery from the very beginning; in fact if I'd left it any longer he may well have begged me to do something about it. He stared at my face and commented, 'You look like Claire Bloom. You've got a heart-shaped face!'

'Sadly, that's just swelling, Jon. It'll go down eventually, but I fear a few wrinkles will reappear,' I replied, realizing that I've grown fond of my swollen state; it's taken years off me.

'I really fancied Claire Bloom,' Jon remarked. 'You don't fancy a fuck, do you?'

I looked at Danielle, his partner of ten years, and rolled my eyes.

This was my first time out and socializing. It did me the world of good to get away from the exclusivity of my own company. Both Jon and Danielle were so supportive and complimentary about my new appearance that seeing them quashed any fears of ridicule I'd had. Jon's seventeen-year-old son also joined us for supper. I've known him since he was seven, an age when he was a morbid creature who always wanted to dissect roadkill. Throughout the meal he didn't notice anything about me, and so at the end I said to him, 'You haven't noticed, have you?'

'Yeah,' he said. 'You've changed your hair colour.'

Without saying a word I lifted my hair and showed him my staples.

'Oh my God, woman! What have you done?' He ran away from the table laughing. I'd finally got him back for years of threats that he was going to dissect their family dog when she passed over.

FRIDAY 5 MARCH 2004

Today I woke up feeling so normal, relaxed, happy, and at peace with myself that I thought, 'Hey, that wasn't so much of a big deal. I could go through it again if that's what it takes to feel confident in myself.' I could tell that today was going to be one of those 'I'm fabulous' days, which are very rare, but enjoyable all the same.

This, on the one hand, is a happy ending. I can only remember two other days in my past when I've been roused from my sleep feeling so at peace with myself. Conversely this is also quite disturbing. If people can experience such positive sensations just twelve days after their operation, no wonder they get addicted to cosmetic improvement. I feel the best I have felt in years. I could almost cry with joy. There's a future ahead of me and a clear horizon. My head is brimming with plans I never dared entertain before. All the anxieties based on concerns about needing 'more time to build my career' and maintaining a 'certain amount of youthfulness' seem to have evaporated, as has the desperate frustration that goes with ambition. It's as if I'm in a car with a full tank of petrol, that's cruising at a gentle speed, and I know I'm going to arrive at my destination on time.

I went to see Dr Olivier de Frahan today at Claridge's, knowing that afterwards I'd be going home to Worcestershire for the first time since Paris. So I was excited by the whole day. I was hopeful that at the very least the stitches in and around the ears would come out and if I was really lucky that all the staples would go too, which would save me from the worry of my mother seeing them by accident. No matter how good a face I had, all she would ever remember and comment on for the rest of her life would be, 'Oh! Those terrible staples ruining your face. What have you done? The end is nigh!'

At Claridge's the doctor was not only running late, but it also seemed as though he was running out of steam.

This guy works so hard, if he could see two patients at once he would. He entered the reception room and told off Debbie, his English PA, for booking the appointments so close together. When he left the room Debbie turned to me, smiled and said, 'That's how he *told* me to do it. He's so rude!' We laughed because even though his manner could easily be mistaken for rudeness, it's all part of his eccentricity. Yes, he is abrupt in a public-schoolboy way, but it never ceases to add to the charm. Then Debbie's mobile rang: it was the doctor, even though he'd just stepped out of the room. He told her he was running twenty minutes late, but had gone outside to take some air. This had me in hysterics, while Debbie was beside herself. Eventually he appeared around a corner and beckoned me into his room.

In the reception room we talked about the Isolagen process, a relatively new technology where skin cells are removed from behind the ear and then grown in a laboratory, later to be injected into the areas of the face that have aged. Apparently it helps to puff up the skin and bring back that youthful roundedness. Everyone wants them but the doctor's response was, 'We do not yet know the outcome – it has not been discovered in the long term.'

I went into his consulting room . . . and the staples came out!

'I am a dressmaker, am I not?' he remarked, as he carefully pulled the staples painlessly from my skin, then held a mirror to the back of my head so I could see his work.

'Couture, I hope. Not off-the-peg?' I asked mischievously.

'Well, of course.'

The doctor didn't get the irony. The streets of Paris aren't lined with the same shops that can be found in every city and town in England and America. In fact the shops, the fashions, the style are unique, and all express the individual in a way that is far-removed from the mass-market 'lookalike' branding that is turning our planet into one big theme park.

So Dr Olivier de Frahan is indeed a couture dress-maker: he's turned this 'second-hand Lil' into a tight little size eight.

After the meeting I drove up to Worcestershire, feeling confident that my face was making a good recovery, and looking forward to being among my friends and family once again.

MONDAY 8 MARCH 2004

At 8 o'clock this morning I was very, very worried. The mirror in front of me wasn't reflecting the image I wanted to see. Under my left eye I could still see a round, prominent swelling, and beneath my right eye there was a pointed lump, exactly as if an internal stitch was fighting to get out. In fact, I wondered whether it could have been caused by inner stitches lifting muscle out of place.

It is exactly two weeks since my operation, and in many ways I should be feeling very lucky. Last month I remembered meeting my close friend, Linda Meredith, who had had her operation in Paris nine weeks previously, and even though she looked fabulous she was noticeably swollen with the 'hamster' look, which I seem to have avoided. For a while one cheek was slightly swollen as if she had a problem with a wisdom tooth, but now three months later she is a new woman, in perfect shape, and any facial swelling has long disappeared over time.

This is what I told myself as I looked in the mirror today. I had no noticeable swelling in the rest of my face, and the little I did have I wanted to keep as it fattened out my face and took years off me. I could walk down the street now and no one would notice or see any unsightly scars, not even the shaven areas behind my ears. But what I did have were two pea-sized lumps under both eyes at the outer corners, which if they were to remain would be difficult to disguise. However, when I pointed them out to the doctor on Friday, he didn't seem at all bothered. In fact he was so pleased that he took his first photo of me, commenting that I had healed with incredible swiftness.

These 'lumps' were a glaring sign that I had had surgery, which was surprising as Dr Olivier de Frahan had a reputation for occasionally repairing the bodged work of other surgeons because all his work was invisible. He insisted I must not touch the area because there were a lot of internal stitches concealed within, and he assured me that in a matter of months they would have corrected themselves. So it's a question of keeping the faith and trusting in him and the healing process. For me the problem is that the rest of the work has gone so well that I do not have the patience to sit out a slow-healing eye.

The small amount of swelling around my face and eyes continues to diminish, which alleviates the tightness I partly love because it has fattened out the wrinkles, but I have long accepted that the area under my eyes has been so bad in the past that it would take a miracle to reduce its tired appearance completely. That said, my eyes are looking 90 per cent better than before the surgery; the skin is smooth and flat, apart from the small lumps at the outer corners. But hey, life is good overall, and after getting up at 5 a.m. and starting work on my one-woman show, my confidence is positively brimming.

* * *

Ha ha! At last I've received a compliment that justifies what I've recently endured for the sake of my face. Later in the day, when I went to stock up at my local Holland and Barrett, one of the women behind the till very innocently cooed over my new hair colour, saying, 'Ooooh, that suits you. You look very distinguished. Stylish. It's changed you completely.' Leaning forward the other one added, 'I hope you don't mind me saying, but you look much better. It's taken years off you!'

Bless them!

One of the many items I gave up in order to detox over the last two months was Diet Coke, and tonight it was all I could think about. I could happily down a litre of the stuff, but I'll be damned if I'm going to give in to this craving. It's not as if it's as spiritually important as chocolate, or even as nutritious. I accept that a litre a day was far too much, and the rumour in the press that it depletes your bones of calcium was all I needed to kick the habit. Instead I drank enough water to float a small flotilla this evening, and as a consequence I slept like a baby.

TUESDAY 9 MARCH 2004

I started the day with the usual inspection routine since the operation, which involves studying my face in minute detail in the bathroom mirror. It strikes me that everything is starting to lift. I can judge this by the fact that for the last two weeks the scars under my eyes have pointed downwards in a sad expression, but today they have lifted to an almost horizontal position. It's a subtle change, but then so is everything about this experience. The healing process is going to take months rather than days.

This morning the pea-sized lump under my left eye was more pronounced. As soon as I massaged it gently in a circular motion it completely disappeared, which baffled me but made me think it was either a muscle in spasm or a trapped nerve or, more worryingly, a suppressed blood vessel. I'm seeing the surgeon in three days' time and I must demand to be put at ease over this. I can't live with it, as it's especially visible when lit from the left, and anyway I'm worried it simply cannot be right. I can't believe this problem is helping the healing process and my fear is that it is hampering the vision in my left eye. When I pointed it out last Friday the surgeon said nothing, and so I accepted that it was simply to be expected, but it seems that it's slowly getting worse and I'd be mad not to act as soon as possible.

That said I feel that I'm looking better all the time. My right eye still has a small and persistent amount of bruising, which drags it down in appearance even though it is rapidly lifting, but once concealer is applied on the bruise it looks wonderful, and the small lump at the outer corner is not as pronounced as the one by the left eye.

My energy levels are astounding me as I truly expected to feel awful for a few weeks, but I am lucky enough to be working from home, which is a double bonus because I am loving it. Although I miss my husband, being alone is a huge benefit. Robert is still in America and won't be back for three days, so all I have to do is look after myself. I'm not surrounded by a vast number of people and so the solitude is exactly what I need to remain focused. I'm sure that if I had to work in an office or look after children or be driving all day I would feel very differently, because if you suddenly hit a brick wall at about 4 p.m., and I usually do, all your strength goes; then you have to surrender to it and settle down for the night.

At 2 p.m. I hit the wall early and had to go to bed for two hours. This took me by surprise but there was no point in fighting it. I slept solidly, waking in the same position in which I'd fallen asleep, on my side with my left hand in a fist under my right ear. Bloody hell! That's not the most sensible thing to do when half your face has been lifted off and re-contoured.

I made myself get up and went out to wake up properly. I think you should only allow yourself so much tiredness, then after that you need to kick-start yourself and fight back.

By 5 p.m. I was back in my study and working hard. There's been some interest from a publisher in America about a children's book I've just started, so I feel that my recovery is aided by the fact my life is going really well. The job offers are many and of a far superior quality than in past years, and consequently it's giving me such a buzz.

I have a telly by my desk and while working I noticed that Richard and Judy were on. Thank God for Richard and Judy, saviours of daytime TV. Put them back on at 10 a.m. – they made the mornings bearable! The subject matter today was footballers, as there had been an alleged rape at a training camp in Spain. Also under discussion was the practice of 'dogging', which I confess I didn't fully understand. I was only half listening when Judy explained that people of a certain persuasion liked to go to outdoor car parks and either have sex themselves or watch sex between consenting strangers.

This made me blush. Last year I was on the road for most of the year in a show and as a non-drinker my way of winding down after an evening's work was to drive to a big open space in the country, turn the CD player up to full volume, get out of the car and dance. I wasn't disturbing anyone and if another car pulled up I'd usually drive off in search of solitude elsewhere. One week I was in Sunderland and couldn't find a car park by the sea that wasn't completely empty. I must have driven to about ten different seaside car parks and they were all relatively full of not only cars but also people milling around, all of whom saw me. It therefore dawned on me that it was highly likely that all these people had been involved in dogging and, what's worse, they may well have thought that I was up for some action too! AARRGGHH!! What would the resulting headlines have done for my career? If I was caught not only dogging but taking cocaine at the same time I would probably get a primetime show on ITV. Unlikely, perhaps, but for some well-known men a bit of controversy has done their careers little harm. Would it work equally for women, I wonder?

There's a stitch on the side of my head I cannot stop fiddling with and now it's sore, which makes me want to touch it even more . . .

WEDNESDAY 10 MARCH 2004

HUGE HUMUNGOUS RELIEF! While staring at my face in the bathroom mirror this morning, I stumbled upon the reason why my left eye keeps pulling down. Hidden in the lashes of my left eye is a stitch that has either been forgotten or left there on purpose. It is so small it looks like an eyelash that has stuck to my lower lid, but upon prodding it with tweezers I discovered that it wouldn't move. Though it'll be a bugger to get out, at least it explains why my eye is slightly distorted in shape, for when I tilt my head downwards or sideways, the eye is restricted by the stitch, pulling on the lower lid as if it is being dragged down by meat hooks. I am so relieved. I find it hard to believe that the doctor could have made any mistake at all with the left eye, as the right is perfect, but the other had troubled me since the op. Now I think that possibly there has been more work done on it, more muscle reconstruction than the right eye, and I can see that once that little stitch is removed the eye will be perfect. YIPPEE! The doctor didn't explain this to me. All he said was, 'Don't touch! The internal stitches are still doing their work.'

For a few minutes I found myself adopting the attitude of a disgruntled consumer: why is my eye a problem? I've paid my bills and so everything should be hunky-dory! Of course it's not like this with surgery; it's impossible to achieve the end result immediately. It's a question of letting time and your body work for it.

Yesterday I was tired all day, which I hated. There is nothing better than finishing your day having done more than you'd expected, but yesterday I managed to write only two pages for my book and I was disappointed. In the evening I made the mistake of having a small whisky, just a single shot to try to help me to sleep as the healing at the back of my ears felt a bit uncomfortable; it had begun to tingle, itch, and sting due to the nerve endings knitting back together.

Whisky and me no longer get on. I used to be able to down half a bottle a day during my school years and still feel normal, but now just the smell knocks the sense out of me. If I can't sleep then I prefer to try a shot of whisky instead of a sleeping pill, but on this occasion I woke up with a dull head, which pissed me off. I didn't want another unproductive day, so I decided that a good long walk to get the blood moving was in order. My body was stale with all this physical rest. The gym was beckoning but the doctor said not for two months, which I'm finding frustrating, but he knows best.

From midday I had my hot-water bottle firmly pressed to my stomach. Pathetic! It took the whole day for my stomach to settle and by 6 p.m. I'd lost hours of work time – GRRRR! In future I will endure a sleepless night rather than experience this kind of reaction to alcohol again. I'm certainly used to getting bouts of nausea every now and again, thanks to having a weak stomach since childhood, but it doesn't get any easier to bear.

Earlier in the day Mum and Dad had come round for morning tea, not knowing I'd been feeling so unwell. Though they had wanted to quiz me about my trip to Paris and talk about the end result, they decided to leave it for another time. Realizing I was severely under the weather there were none of the usual guilt trips being played out either; my father didn't mention his visits to the doctor for all his various and imagined ills, and my mother didn't nag about the usual things, from my handwriting to Robert's lengthy absences. I might be as strong as an ox and as hard as a traffic warden, but mess with my well-balanced constitution and I'm buggered for twenty-four hours.

For the past few days the area around all the cut surfaces of my face has become sore to the touch for the first time. This is good, as it means that feeling is returning. There has also been the bizarre phenomenon of phantom itches, when I want to scratch an itch in an area that is still numb. The side of my face suddenly develops an itch, but I cannot feel a thing when I scratch it. Then the area starts to tingle as if little mites are trooping the colour around my face. I suppose that this must all be part of the healing process, and that my nerves are knitting themselves together again, but these are by far the most distracting sensations yet.

Though I've been spared any real pain, I now have 'low-watt' electricity dancing across my face, which makes it a little hard to sleep. Not only that but last night the 'tide' of tinnitus kept going in and out of my right ear. I felt as if I was at a dance club. I even got out of bed twice to see if someone was knocking at the front door, the blood in my ear was pounding so deafeningly. Thankfully it's gone now.

THURSDAY 11 MARCH 2004

My friend and confidant Ruby came over for lunch today at my Worcestershire home. Ruby is a gay man who prefers to dress as a woman when he's out on the town, but today he's all man in Vivienne Westwood. Not only do I not have a clue as to the most politically correct term for his 'lifestyle' choice, but I don't give a damn and neither does he. It's none of my business anyway. Ruby likes dresses, Ruby likes men; I like trousers, I like men; the important thing is that we like each other. Every woman should have a gay best friend because their advice on clothes, colours, soft furnishings and holidays is always the best, and when I'm out with Ruby I know

I'm going to have a good time. He's a hostess in his own nightclub in Stoke, and he advises me on my stage costumes, my accountants, my choice of car, and how to deal with my mother, and he never tells me when I've put on weight. Perhaps every woman should marry a gay man and just have casual affairs. THAT'S IT! The secret to a long and happy life!

When he arrived I revealed my scars to him with great excitement, as enthusiastically as a woman showing off her newborn child, or a man when his new car is delivered. It was the first time that Ruby had seen me since Paris, and I was expecting more interest from him than I initially received.

At the sight of the back of my head, Ruby grimaced. 'That looks sore!'

'No, it's just dye,' I replied.

Nothing more was said on the subject, and I didn't push it. I was itching to ask him, 'Well, what do you think?' but Ruby wasn't interested any more. The moment passed and we moved on to his boyfriend situation; Paris was consigned to history.

Halfway through lunch I blurted out, 'Well, what do you think? Do I look better?' Then I realized that he'd just needed time to assess my appearance.

'Yes, you can see what he's done. Your eyes look very different. You're obviously still a bit swollen, so it's hard to judge yet,' he replied honestly.

Sensible answer. He wasn't ignoring the work, he was simply studying it. Ruby has a habit of following in my footsteps like a younger sister, but I somehow think that a facelift will be one step too far for him.

Ruby has no desire to become a woman. He is comfortable in his male body and doesn't appear to associate beauty with the face in the way that I do. He is lucky in that he has fantastic legs, and when he goes 'female' he shows this asset off in fishnet tights to such levels of success that he's even managed to have flings with straight men, from night-club bouncers to those of the married variety. Yes, Ruby has been both a gangster's moll and a mistress.

Beauty for Ruby is a small waist, curvy hips and a high bust line, everything you'd expect a 1950s film star would need to bring her success. To him, the face is something that can be disguised with make-up, and because of this Ruby has never had a problem with switching between male and female, as beauty can be applied to this part of the body. In the ten years I have known him he has never once voiced concerns about age or wasted time worrying about what he hasn't got. He doesn't suffer from the 'if only I had bigger boobs and higher eyebrows' syndrome. Ruby is masculine in his confidence and feminine in his expression, and has the best of both worlds. But because he has seen what I have done to myself to alleviate the signs of ageing, from Botox to diet to surgery, I can sense that he is wondering whether to follow suit.

Being anxious about his frown lines, which look more masculine when he wears a female wig, he's already booked to see my Botox man, Dr Patrick Bowler, even though I've tried to persuade him he really doesn't need to. However, I'd rather he went to Patrick, who is a leading dermatologist, than to a novice in a high-street shop.

One of the hardest things about having had plastic surgery is that you realize that you're a walking advert for the stuff. It's a hell of a responsibility knowing that if you look great and have got through the procedure comfortably, others will follow suit. But no matter how well it goes for one person, it is still always a gamble for another, and the thought that my happiness could lead to another's displeasure is a heavy burden to bear. I am now telling all my friends that if they want to go through with it, they should do it by their rules, choose who's right for them and follow their instincts, because even though they are putting their life in another person's hands, the decision is theirs alone, and only they should carry that responsibility.

Surgery is incredibly personal. Although I have complained in earlier pages that I felt wronged as a result of the negative comments I've received from men, the main motivation for having it done was to please myself. I don't believe that anyone but Toyah Willcox could have persuaded me to do it. For example, if my husband had suggested it or my management had really pushed for it, I would have left my hubby and got a new manager. No one has the right to tell anyone to alter their body, in fact I'd go as far to say that it would be criminal if they did. Perhaps I am over-sensitive, but I worried myself sick before I had the operation and I wouldn't wish that on anyone. Yes, I could argue that I'm now the happiest I've been in twenty years, but this is my life, not yours; only you know your needs and the reactions of those around you. It is also possible that surgery could cause too much friction in a relationship; I've heard men say they would leave their wives if they even had Botox. So many elements have to be considered before having any sort of procedure, and my success is no reason to go right ahead without giving proper thought to the possible consequences.

Ruby and I were in a quiet respectable restaurant, in the midst of ladies who lunch. I had no idea how, but we got on to the subject of 'dogging', and I told Ruby about my strange passion for driving to remote spots, in order to turn the radio up and get out and dance in the great outdoors, which, in my ignorance had led to many a quick getaway from shaking bushes and inquisitive drivers who had annoyed me with their flashing car lights. Ruby laughed and told me unprintable things that made me realize I'd somehow managed to miss out on a whole new movement, as it seems that dogging is going on at every level in most car parks up and down the country.

Dogging? 'So *passé*. So *de trop*,' said Ruby, giving me a wicked smile. I should have known.

FRIDAY 12 MARCH 2004

I was in London today to see the doctor and the timing couldn't have been better. My left eye was frightening me as the muscles seemed to be bunching up in the lower inner corner. If I kept my head angled slightly upwards I looked normal, but once I dipped my head it pulled down and looked like something out of a horror film. The prospect of walking around holding my head up for the rest of my life doesn't really appeal. In fact it dulls my enthusiasm for anything. Are there any horror films being cast at the moment? I bet no actress has gone to these extremes to get a job looking scary.

Dr Olivier de Frahan was late, but I forgave him. He works his arse off and it wasn't his fault if Eurostar had a hiccup. He looked dashing today: blue velvet jacket and a flick in the floppy fringe that made him seem especially debonair. The cynic in me wondered which supermodel was due in his surgery today.

I had a lot of questions to ask him and was determined to get some sort of acknowledgement that my eye needed checking. One of this doctor's many exceptional qualities is registering someone's anxiety in seconds, so I didn't have to huff and puff to get him to pay my eye full attention; I had it the moment I entered the room.

'Now why is it doing that?' he asked himself.

We established that the muscles were playing up and that I needed to massage the eye, to re-educate the muscles to sit properly around the actual eyeball. He showed me what to do, by gently using two fingers moving upwards against the muscle, and he asked me to use eye-drops containing a steroid. He also noticed there was still a lot of swelling in the general area.

I was relieved that it could be treated in London. The thought of returning to Paris for more work would have been really bad news.

I remained convinced that I still had a stitch in my left eyelid, but after searching for it he couldn't find one. In fact it turned out to be an in-growing eyelash, which wouldn't be the cause of my eyelid pulling down. This disappointed me as I wanted something I could see to be the cause, not something else that was internal, which I could not comprehend. I must admit that I was a little tense about it all, especially as it became evident that this part of the process relied only on time.

'You have internal stitches still, that is what those small bumps are. They will dissolve by the end of May,' he assured me. 'Also, your left eye will improve all the time.'

It takes strength to trust in the notion that time will heal, as there are no guarantees other than the doctor's confidence and experience. Though I am reassured, I still don't have solid proof that I won't have to walk around with my head up for the rest of my life.

As the time for me to return to work was fast approaching, there were a few things I needed to know, so I put a number of questions to the doctor. Concerned as I was about the possible effect of dye or bleach making contact with my scars, I asked whether I could dye my hair, and I was told that in a week's time indeed I could, but I mustn't allow any peroxide on the scars.

When could I exercise? I could begin to start exercising again in another week, but I mustn't do any high-impact workouts for a year. At this stage exercise would only encourage the muscles to drop, and I certainly didn't want to add to gravity in pulling the skin down, as it needed to be tricked into pulling up.

When can I have Botox again? I was informed that I could have it any time, but there was no need to have it around the crow's feet at the side of my eyes because they will have gone for good. Apparently, when the swelling has completely gone down, my eye area will be smooth, without any sign of puffiness.

SATURDAY 13 MARCH 2004

Robert returned from the US yesterday, and we reunited happily in Worcestershire. It's fantastic to have him back. He's noticed an incredible difference since he last saw me, twelve days ago, and told me, 'You look superb!'

As time goes by my skin is feeling tighter. This has both its benefits and its downsides. I love the feeling of tightness and it gives me tons of confidence, but I am still slightly swollen and the tightness is causing my eyes to drag down. The left eye is hellish and embarrassing. I find that I'm massaging it all day rather than for the five minutes that the doctor ordered.

Now I know why it is said that week three is the 'why did I do it?' week. I'm itchy and the swelling has gone down enough to make me look like a forty-five-year-old again. As a consequence, what also emerged was the path of the surgeon's remoulding just under my ears. I could see the route taken by his instruments where he had lifted the skin and repositioned it. It's not terrible and only I know what it is, but the skin around the ear and neck feels hard and angry, almost leathery. In bed last night Robert's head was on my pillow when he remarked that he could see where the surgeon had worked on my neck.

It became evident today that I was entering my first bad phase; a time of questioning where the seed of doubt had been cast over my actions. I was beginning to understand why the doctor had told me that the whole journey takes six months, during which time steady improvements are constantly being made. All these subtleties that are bothering me need to fade away.

Because the skin on my neck is hard to the touch I tried putting a generous layer of Crème de la Mer over the area. It helped, but I think my face swelled as a result of being a little sensitive to anything other than air. I remembered the post-operative care assistant telling me that 'essential oils will cause a reaction', so I decided not to do that again, for a while at least.

Apart from this I was in good spirits. With Robert back home it is a lovely time for us both. His homecoming always excites me and today I felt at peace with the world. He slept till midday, jetlagged. When I woke him with a mug of Earl Grey he looked at me and said, 'Is this my wife?'

'Do I look different?' I asked.

'It's the hair I'm getting used to,' he replied.

A lot of people think that not only is my hair different, but that I have also lost weight. I don't tell them otherwise.

Robert and I went to the supermarket and I decided to show off for him. I did a mad disco dance down the aisles in celebration of the Bee Gees playing over the tannoy, two packets of biscuits in one hand and a can of baked beans in the other, shimmying past the breakfast cereals like Carmen Miranda. When I turned to see his reaction I discovered he had hidden behind some shelves and left me dancing to the Muzak completely on my own. The bastard! I smiled politely at all the passing shoppers and went in search of the wee Sassenach.

My period came early today. I thought this might happen, as it's not surprising that a serious op should throw your cycle out of kilter. Consequently I was gaga with tiredness by 9 p.m. and Robert sent me to bed, as I was a danger to myself and all around me. It's as if I hit a brick wall: one minute I'm chatting away, the next I'm dribbling.

I didn't feel quite human today, more like an organism that keeps on living, breathing, eating and sleeping even though it has been tampered with. My body is in a constant state of readjustment. I'm not quite me. I'm just an organism among billions on the face of the planet, except this one has made some attempt to change itself.

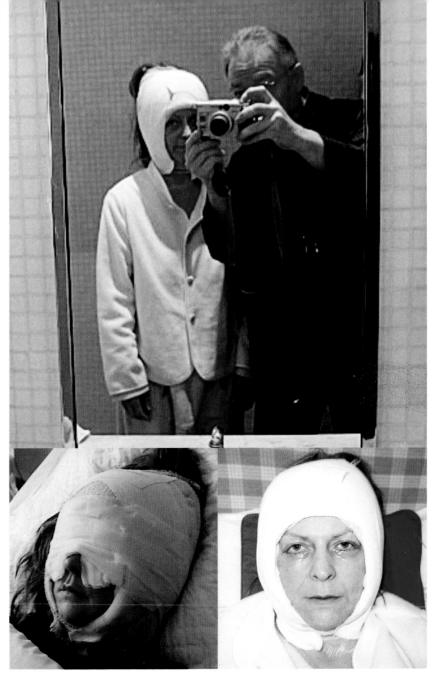

With my husband Robert (*top*), the official photographer for the whole adventure and an incalculable source of support. As cosmetic surgery procedures become increasingly popular, couples are starting to take the journey together.

In the hospital recovery room, five hours after the operation on 23 February 2004 (*above left*); back 'home' at the hotel the next day, but there's still a long way to go (*above right*). The following week is the most unglamorous of my life, but it's worth every minute for the end results.

Above: I am not the most patient of patients! Alleviating the boredom of convalescence by doing some light ballet exercises by the bed two days after my surgery.

Below: I was lucky that my recuperation was relatively problem-free: only my eyes kept giving me grief. Here, Dr Olivier de Frahan has instructed me to adhere to a regime of eye-patches and cold compresses for a while, in order to aid my rehabilitation.

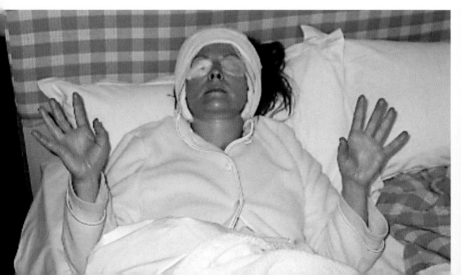

Above: Four days later I'm on the road to recovery and (*above right*) 'dressing up' to meet the outside world for the first time since the op. Would you have recognized me?

Below: After six days my eyes are already beginning to transform into an attractive shape.

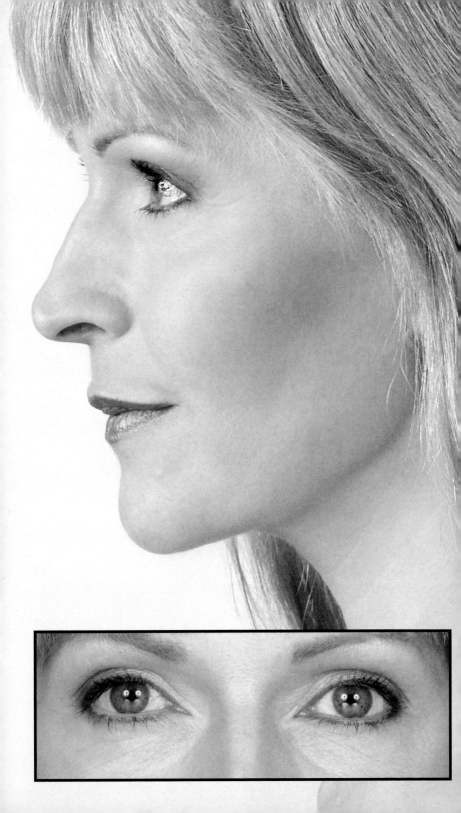

Facing page: Eleven weeks on from the operation. I look ten years younger, the scars are invisible and my eyes (*inset*) are smooth again for the first time in twenty years. I am delighted with the results.

This page: Looking forward to a bright future.

Trying on my new costume for an eighties-revival show (*above*); and cheering on the crowd at a recent gig (*inset*).

Posing for the 'Here and Now'
tour (*above*); feeling fabulous
and looking great (*right*).

Overleaf: Life has never been so good.

SUNDAY 14 MARCH 2004

Eyes! Eyes! My eyes!
Windows to my soul.
Broadcasting who I am to the rest of the world.
Harbingers of dreams to the outer world.
Vessels that hold pain and joy.
Bright. Brilliant. Jewel-like green.
Green with jealousy; green with envy; green with
seduction; green with love; green with pride.

Today my eyes were an absolute pain. I could have plucked them out and stuck them on cocktail sticks in the fridge. Dry, itchy and drooping; two little bastards poking fun at me!

My hair was thick and sticky with a week's worth of grime and I wanted to wash it the way I always do, by submerging my head under water in a hot bath, not by showering; so I did. But in doing this I caused even more irritation to my eyes and the muscles seemed to tighten in reaction. Now both eyes were pulling down, which made it hard to be optimistic about them ever being right again.

My eyes were my power source, my Samson's hair; now I feared they were purely functional, rather than captured stars or jewels of the sea.

Mum and Dad came to supper and Robert and I talked them through the photos that we'd taken in Paris after the operation. All the pictures had a morbid similarity as they played in sequence on Robert's computer on the kitchen table, but seeing them allowed my parents to understand. My mother was especially intrigued, and though criticism usually came before compliments, I could tell by her interest that it was something she would have considered if she were younger. For quite a while she became a different person as she studied the pictures. There were no disparaging remarks, only inquisitive questions and gasps of horror.

My mother is now in her late seventies, but when she was in her forties she followed the 1970s trend to let go of her youth. At that time, to be in one's forties was to be middle-aged, and my mother simply accepted this, which is not something that my generation is doing. Her dress sense remains immaculate, but like many women of her age, my mother opted out of remaining youthful. Stopping middle-age spread is an art form and a full-time commitment, which in those days held such novelty value that Joan Collins, Jane Fonda and Zsa Zsa Gabor appeared daily in the press on account of their age-defying abilities. My mother lived during a period when the image of youthful perfection didn't dominate our screens the way it does now. So as we sat around the kitchen table I could tell she was experiencing my journey through her eyes. I was sure that she would have done the same at my age if the choice had been available to her. My mother is one of the most beautiful women I have ever seen, in particular (and most ironically) when she was in her forties. I remember when she took me to my first 'boys included' party when I was thirteen and the boy I'd decided to kiss that night saw my mum, turned to his male pals and said, 'Cor, who's that? I'd like to snog her!' I never got kissed that night.

She scrutinized every photo and asked question after question: 'Did this hurt? Why are those stitches there? Why are your eyes bandaged? What did it cost? Did you really wear the same nightgown for eight days? How could you?' For about twenty minutes she had escaped into my world, and divorced herself from the critical human being that I know her to be, but that she herself doesn't acknowledge. It didn't take long for her to change back though.

'I hope this won't make your eyes smaller,' she remarked.

It seems that no matter how good I look, my mother will always find a reason to criticize. If, by any miracle, I ever win an Oscar, I could bring it home and put it on the mantelpiece and she would start to fret over the chances of it being stolen.

'Do they look smaller?' I asked.

'No. I just hate it when you see women with piggy eyes from having had plastic surgery.'

'He's made mine bigger.'

'Really? Well, I hope they don't get smaller.'

Mum didn't even look at me as she uttered these last words, which fell effortlessly from her mouth. She was just running one of her many, many, too-many-to-mention fears, on automatic. Dad gave me the 'ignore her' expression, while in contrast he looked over the moon. He'd been hinting that I needed my eyes done since I was twenty-five, and so he wasn't concerned if it had hurt or if it had been expensive; he just wanted me to look good on TV.

Somehow we got on to the subject of the Osbournes. My father had never seen them on television, so I tried to describe them as best I could without using the obligatory f-word too often. Then Mum said surprisingly, 'Oh, I do like Sharon Osbourne. She's such a lovely woman.'

This was indeed a noteworthy event. In God knows how many years, I had never heard my mother say anything nice about anyone, especially another woman. Even after Robert takes her out for the day, and treats her to lunch and the cinema, praise does not fall from her lips. It's always doom and gloom. So I was amazed that the one person in the world she chooses to be nice about is Sharon Osbourne, who just so happens to be my heroine because she kicks arse! I wonder if I could introduce her to my mother . . .

MONDAY 15 MARCH 2004

This morning it struck me that the weekend had disappeared so quickly I felt as though it had been stolen. On Friday I'd bought two books to read as research for certain projects I am planning: Zoë Heller's *Notes On A*

Scandal and Martina Cole's *The Know*. Well, I picked *Notes On A Scandal* up on Friday evening and had finished it by last night. PHUT! Two days gone while I was in a heavenly oblivion of words. How can a book do that to you and so easily steal your precious hours? Every line was like a drug that drove me on, and I couldn't get enough of it. It was sheer pleasure. If I came across books like that every other day my life would be over in a flash.

In accordance with the doctor's instructions, I continued to massage my left eye in order to improve the pulling-down effect. It felt as if the skin was malleable, like clay that could be manipulated into its correct shape or, in this case, its proper position. I suppose really it is a case of educating the muscles beneath, as the discomfort is being caused by their contraction, almost as if the muscles are having one hell of a rebellion under the skin of the left eye. Therefore the massage is to tell them to relax, to chill out.

I'm relieved to see that the scar tissue is fading at a rate of knots to match the rest of my skin tone. I'm not sure if this has come about through the passing of time or whether the Eight Hour ointment from Elizabeth Arden that I've been applying around the top of my neck and behind the ears (where my skin feels hard) has been having a magic effect. I'm sure it's a sophisticated version of Hypercal, but it's an ointment rather than a cream, and is a remedy for all skin conditions. It really does the trick. I was introduced to it by all the make-up artists with whom I've worked over the years. They swore by its healing qualities when rubbed on lips and skin blemishes. Sîan Lloyd chose it as the one luxury item she wanted to take into the jungle on *I'm A Celebrity, Get Me Out Of Here!* and we would all be queueing to use it in the mornings!

By 8.30 a.m. I found that I'd spent an hour texting back and forth to Danniella Westbrook, who told me how proud she was that I'd had a facelift. Previously she had had reconstructive surgery to rebuild the septum in her nose after recovering from cocaine addiction. When I first met her in the jungle we briefly touched upon the subject of her nasal surgery, but I didn't like to ask too much as she had already had to contend with an unnecessary level of press intrusion on arriving in Australia. The paparazzi were positioned on the rooftops of the surrounding buildings when we were based at the hotel, both before and after the programme, and there were occasions when we had had to shield her and her children from the cameras. Danniella is quite happy to talk about her past life, though, especially if it deters others from taking drugs.

I'd first encountered her while we were at a London fashion show in 1992, when she was an up-and-coming star. She was sensationally beautiful and breathtakingly innocent. That day she was accompanied by three other young members of the *EastEnders* cast, one of whom asked me if I had any cocaine. Though it wasn't an unusual request in the world of show business, it wasn't one I expected to hear from a teenager. I thought nothing more of it, and put it down to the naive enthusiasm of teenage fame, until I read the stories associated with the drug-taking that would make Danniella infamous. I didn't meet her again until our jungle experience in April 2003, but was pleased to see that she was still beautiful. We have remained close. She has said that I'm the double of her mother and I must admit I feel maternally protective towards her.

At Christmas 2003 she came to see the show I was doing in Canterbury, and it was while she was snuggling into the sofa in my dressing room that I told her I was planning a facelift in Paris.

'You can't go to just anyone. I'll find someone for you,' she said.

'Well, I'm happy with whom I have in mind; it's the anaesthetic that scares me.'

Danniella had had her last breast enlargement just a

week earlier, and so I asked her how she had coped with so many anaesthetics in such a short period of time.

'I tell them to give me as little as is needed,' she replied. 'You know, Toyah, I have a problem with my nose and I can't have tubes everywhere. When you meet the anaesthetist you must insist on having as little anaesthetic as possible, just the minimum to keep you under.'

'Do you worry when you have surgery?' I asked, 'because I'm having sleepless nights over this.'

'No, but I haven't had anything as big as you're about to go through. It doesn't worry me at all because I know and trust my surgeon. He's the best.'

That time in my dressing room really put me at ease. Even Danniella's husband, Kevin, was supportive: 'Paris sounds right. I've heard they do good work there.'

Danniella's recent breast enlargement had been a Christmas present from her husband, and it was clear that they were both delighted with the outcome. They accentuated her tiny waist and made her look more girlish than ever. In a way I could understand the desire for new boobs when you're in an industry flooded with young girls who treat them as the latest fashion accessory, but at what point do you decide they are big enough?

Why would she consider surgery when she was perfect in the first place? It's her choice, of course. Not all naturally beautiful people have inner confidence, and in Danniella's case having surgery obviously makes her feel better about herself, which can only be a good thing.

Three months later and we were exchanging messages about the success of my own surgery, which filled me with pride and relief in equal measure.

TUESDAY 16 MARCH 2004

Yesterday Dr Olivier de Frahan faxed me the details of the product he wants me to put in my eye, but because it contains a small amount of steroids it must first be given the all-clear by my GP. Fortunately permission has been granted and it's OK for me to use, but at the chemist's there was none in stock and it had to be ordered.

Just as the doctor told me it would, my eye is responding to the massage, which has also reduced the swelling noticeably. This makes me think I should be massaging the rest of my face as well, as I'm looking slightly hamsterish, like Sarah Brightman sucking an aniseed ball.

It was a normal day today. My skin felt tight, a little tighter than I've been used to, but it wasn't a problem. I carried on with my work, wishing I could properly return to the outside world, but I still felt a little slow.

WEDNESDAY 17 MARCH 2004

My mood, thoughts and opinions have been swinging backwards and forwards like a pendulum, from being cheery and light-hearted to dark and despairing. I must be in what they call the 'Oh my God, what have I done?' stage. My skin is tight, there's an increase in water retention all over my face, and my eyes are dry and at the point of itching. For all my worrying in the past month I've never really been so panicked that I've regretted my decision, but now after three weeks, I'm expecting to wake up to improvements not setbacks, which is what it has started to feel like.

These past three days have been a blissful retreat in the company of Robert, who has been administering Grade-A attention, but deep down I am a workhorse and not a princess. The novelty of being at home is wearing off and daytime TV can only offer so much companionship and entertainment. I want to be part of the entertainment world in an active sense again, not sitting here watching it passively. It seems that the lack of work-related stress is like a slow withdrawal from a drug to which one is happy to be addicted.

[167]

When I had my first meeting in London with the doctor in December 2003, I can remember being quietly shocked at a discussion I overheard between two middle-aged women in the reception area, in which one was singing the praises of all the treatments and minor enhancements she had had at various other clinics around London. 'You must try this . . . You must try that . . . Go to so and so . . .' etc. etc.

It dawned on me that all these two women probably did with their time was have beauty treatments. They were Middle Eastern in appearance, so not surprisingly I presumed they were the wives of wealthy oil sheiks living out a cliché. Feeling no guilt as I listened to every word, I entered into a daydream about what it would be like to have nothing to do but spend someone else's money all day. It would be a novelty of gossamer weight, surely, and I imagine the joy of it would last about a week before a paranoid notion of having been 'bought to be an ornament' would take over. These women had a lot to talk about and a need to be heard, and after five minutes it was evident that they only had each other as sounding posts, and I imagined that once they were home they had to revert back to the role of wife and mother, and temporarily suspend their passion for pampering.

Having absorbed a very long list of all the treatments they'd experienced, from hair removal to various laser processes, one would have expected them to look like supermodels or at the very least well rested and glowing. But they didn't. Instead they looked like average, tired, overweight women, which suggested to me that despite everything they'd tried, they still couldn't overcome some hidden anxiety. They were in the same situation as I was, because no matter how much I dieted, exercised, gave up caffeine, alcohol, sugar, fat, carbohydrates and chocolate, I still couldn't improve my looks. Some of us simply have to take extreme action. Just like me, they needed to engage the help of someone who would erase the anxiety of life from their faces. The only difference between us was that they were fabulously wealthy with time on their hands, and I was a career girl intent on extending my working life for as long as I was able.

I left that appointment in December in a state of joy at being over-pressured and overworked. After all, Christmas is a time of everyday matinees and three hours of press interviews each morning – pantoland needs me. The thought of a two-hour drive before doing two shows seemed like a gift. It's ironic that while my mind loves stress, my body hates it. Looking back at those busy pre-op days I realize that I was in a very different emotional place then to the one in which I find myself today, enduring this enforced post-op respite. The last three weeks have been greatly appreciated as a rare but necessary interval in a thirty-year career, but now I've had enough, and I'm desperate to get back to what I am used to most – a life of pressure and deadlines.

At midday today the phone rang. Could I go out on tour with *Calamity Jane* in seven months' time? Ah, that old friend panic reared up its head once more. Would I be fit enough? Would the physical stress ruin my face again? Did I want to put myself through the same gruelling schedule as before? Just last week I had been given assurances that this musical, which I have worked on for the last two years, wasn't going to be resurrected until spring 2005. I was quietly relieved to hear this as I didn't feel strong enough currently to throw myself into what is in fact a thinly disguised marathon. Having been under the impression that time was on my side, I had already verbally committed to touring with Nick Heyward in October. After much debate with producers, tour managers and directors, however, it seemed that, if necessary, the producers of *Calamity Jane* would release me for that period, as long as I returned after the series of rock concerts.

I love working and I enjoy the challenge of hard graft,

but the thought of going from *Calamity* to a rock tour, back to *Calamity,* then straight into panto seems like madness. Though the spirit and body might be willing, I'm not convinced my voice will be, as *Calamity* put it in a permanent state of squeak. What with all the moving around I had to do while singing, combined with the accent I had to adopt, it was like a contortionists' convention. Another serious point I had to consider was that the reason I had a facelift in the first place was because the exhausting *Calamity* experience had put years on me. Will I be ready for three months of high-impact physical activity? Will all the internal stitching be strong enough by then? Or will everything stretch and sag?

For the last three months of the two-year run of *Calamity Jane*, when we were based in the West End, I really wasn't happy, which I think was part of the reason that my face went south last year. London's Theatreland had been in a sorry state back then: there were no tourists and there was a heatwave. Consequently our production suffered, as did many other shows in the capital. I found this very distressing, and felt a personal responsibility towards the theatre, the cast and the producer, as we had all worked our socks off for more than a year to get the show where it was.

Everything was disheartening at this time, except the audiences who seemed to be on a morale-boosting mission. The critics were split and honest about the show's shortcomings – admittedly it is dated, sexist and laughably racist – but worst of all they were unforgivably personal, and took relish in tearing me apart. I had never felt so harshly treated in my life and it broke my heart that a superb young cast had to be dragged down in my name. As a result all these negative feelings had etched themselves on my face and I wanted to erase them and the associated memories. I know the show will work in the provinces whenever it tours again, as regional theatre is on a high, and enjoys even greater attendances than the

West End. But as far as my role is concerned, I have to think long and hard when considering the damage I could do to myself, both physically and mentally.

On top of all this, the day got livelier and livelier. Five years ago Robert and I moved from our long-standing home in Wiltshire. We packed up all our beloved art, sculptures and furniture, placed them in storage, and didn't put roots down again until two and half years ago. Today all the garden statues from our old house were erected for the first time since we settled in Worcestershire and it feels like we've truly established our roots again. It's a lovely feeling.

My eye-drops arrived at last, and they had an immediate effect. Slowly my left eye is behaving and I can see that my facial swelling needs to reduce to reveal whether the eye will continue to pull down. I don't think it will. I think it's a combination of the lower swelling in the face dragging everything down, and a muscle in spasm. Things are improving slowly.

We are now entering the Dark of the Moon, which are the three days before new moon. They are sacred days for me and I reserve them for creativity. I try not to succumb to any distractions to ensure that nothing interferes with my life during these hours as they are considered to be important times of perception. New moon is significant in my life as it symbolizes the start of new beginnings and fresh insight. Any idea or dream I have during this period I take very seriously; luckily I'm not dreaming of wonky eyes or chins falling onto laps any more! Instead I allow myself to be creative. The results are always surprising, and it's almost as if these days offer people the chance to tap into a pool of creativity which is available to all those who bother to look for it.

This month and next will be a time reserved for writing my one-woman show. Tonight I got the first ten pages down and it put butterflies in my stomach. It felt plausible. It felt good.

THURSDAY 18 MARCH 2004

I need to get fit. My usually muscular body has become puny. They say you put weight on when you have plastic surgery because of the lack of exercise, but I seem to be shrinking. This could be an opportunity to reduce my leg muscles, which to me are like great shanks of beef that could feed the world or frighten intruders. I'm very small in stature but have a body that muscle-builders would die for. Perhaps with muscle shrinkage I could get myself better proportioned.

Yesterday my acting agent told me that my voice sounded restricted and strained. I thought this was an odd thing to say, but afterwards I realized he was probably worrying that the facelift or the tightening of the neck had restricted my vocal cords. I didn't think so. I'd told the doctor I was a vocalist before the treatment, and he said he didn't imagine there would be any such problems in this regard.

I've decided not to carry on waiting for the passing of time to drain the excess fluid from my face. Instead, I will attempt to give myself a lymphatic-drainage massage each morning, as the care assistant in Paris had showed me what to do. I hadn't imagined that it would be something I'd have to do to get the swelling down, as I'd presumed it would disappear by itself. But no, the puffiness is constant and ever changing, and not showing any sign of disappearing. So when I wake up I gently massage my face in outward and upward moves for half an hour. I began the procedure yesterday morning for the first time, and after just two sessions it's working; the swelling is reducing. I know that as soon as I stop it will all come back again, so I will have to sustain this activity indefinitely, or for a few weeks at least.

The lymphatic-drainage practitioner used to tell me that the 'corpse' responds to the gentlest of pressure applied to the face and neck, which enables the excess fluid to drain into the lymphatic system in the shoulders.

'The "corpse"?' I asked her, the first time she mentioned the unusual word.

'Oh, I am sorry. Body!' she replied.

Sometimes I feel like a corpse . . .

Today was a good day. By 7 a.m. I had written thirty pages (the first fifteen minutes) of *Chain Reaction*, my one-woman show, and it felt great to be making good progress with it. Having woken up at 4 a.m. I decided that rather than lie in bed feeling bored I would get up and do some work. So I went to my desk and began to write, stopping every now and then to look out of my study window, and watch street cleaners and milkmen go about their daily business.

FRIDAY 19 MARCH 2004

Today was the first day when the skin at the back of my ear and just under the lobe on the neck actually felt like real skin. Previously it had felt like coarse, dead leather that's been left on a stove to dry after a rainfall. As well as being numb, it had also seemed like it didn't belong to me any more. To me it was the texture of this area of skin that gave away the fact it had been 'lifted' and repositioned. Luckily it has begun to feel alive again. It looks fine, albeit a little hot and bluish, but it's settling nicely.

I've taken to gently tapping the skin around my ears because I am having phantom itches that are caused by the nerves knitting. There is nothing more stomach-churning than trying to scratch an itch on numb skin; you feel like a ghost that's dreaming it's alive.

My one-woman show is thrilling me. I've started to get up at 4 a.m. each day to write while the world is still quiet. The project is growing into something I never expected: mad, wacky and technically adventurous. I pray we can find a remote-controlled armchair, as this has somehow become 50 per cent of the show. It needs to be able to dance and have a mind of its own. Puppet strings will not do and neither will two men with long ropes positioned on either side of the stage pulling this 'gravity-defying' chair in every direction!

There is an air of rediscovered confidence about myself and I put that all down to the operation. This is partly because I found the strength within myself to go through with it, and partly because I now feel I can let go of the anxiety that surrounds my looks and image. Having said that, I'm still concerned that my eyes haven't sorted themselves out yet. They are a never-ending source of grief and are severely testing my faith at the moment, especially when both eyes are playing up. Last night my right eye was so sore that I turned into a complete ratbag.

Today I have noticed that sometimes both eyes are fine, even the left, but then something underneath the skin (it could be muscle), will tighten on both eyes and pull them down as if there is a puppeteer within me pulling little strings attached to the skin and distorting my face. At certain times I have a look of wide-eyed innocence, which is almost appealing, then my eyes seem to be pulled downwards a stage further, which produces a look of premature ageing, similar to the droop on the face of a ninety-year-old. Because there are moments when they behave it is possible to believe that they will be all right in time, and that it's all part of the ever-elusive healing process. For instance the pea-sized lump I had all last week which swelled and then disappeared when massaged has now completely gone. But all the rest is really testing my patience.

SATURDAY 20 MARCH 2004

The swelling around my cheekbones is reducing slowly but comfortably. The scars under the eyes are turning from an angry pink colour to match my skin tone and have almost disappeared. It is the same for the scars around the ears. My left ear scar is invisible thanks to the doctor's efforts to cut slightly into the ear area, and my right scar, which is more visible, is slowly turning skin-toned too.

My eyes are still driving me to distraction, however. I read the instructions on the packet of eye-drops and learned that one of the possible side effects is irritation. As a dyslexic I rely almost exclusively on visual information and so to have this sense restricted is akin to suffering a minor stroke. It's hideous. My movement, spelling and balance are up the spout. I feel as though I'm on the waltzer at a fairground and I can't get off.

Yesterday, while cleaning my teeth, I realized that a lower crown was loose, so today I went to the dentist to have it fixed. Because I didn't want a Novocaine injection, which I was afraid might cause an adverse facial reaction, I informed the dentist that I'd just had surgery. He continued with his work without administering any painkillers.

'Was it a general anaesthetic?' he asked me.

'Yes. Why?'

'Sometimes the tubes they use can knock your teeth.'

When he eventually removed the crown, which took quite some time to extract even though it was loose, he discovered that it had been rooted into my jaw using six pins.

'Whoever set this tooth did a very good job,' he remarked admiringly.

'What could have loosened it then?' I asked, quite puzzled.

'One hell of a knock,' he replied.

I knew for a fact that this couldn't have been the case, otherwise there would have been considerable bruising on that part of my face. For the first four days after surgery I hadn't been able to open my jaw. Now I wondered whether they might have had to clamp my jaw open. Nothing is ever as simple or as straightforward as you think it's going to be when you have the preliminary meetings with the surgeon, but the more I find out about the possible things that could have taken place during the operation, the more I want to know exactly what did occur.

SUNDAY 21 MARCH 2004

It's Mothering Sunday. The church bells are pealing, the sun is glorious and spring is finally here!

Every morning for the past three days I have been attempting to give myself lymphatic-drainage massage around the face, and it appears to be taking effect. The sensation is coming back to the skin around the ears and the shape definition is returning, but still that damned left eye is dragging down. When I see the doctor next I am going to have to insist on taking immediate action. I don't think he understands that it'll give the press a golden opportunity to jump on the 'look what she's done to herself!' bandwagon if it isn't sorted out quickly.

It really pisses me off as everything else is so perfect. Why the hell is this eye playing up? I really need reassurances and guarantees now. If I were brave enough I'd just go with it and see if time will work things out. Who knows, if it doesn't repair itself it could even lead to more work. Imperfect, quirky or 'character' looks have a value in my industry too. After all, if it's beauty we all strive for, how do those who will never achieve the sociably perfect look manage? They can go to the other extreme and find infamy instead. I remember reading film reviews in the 1970s featuring claims that during the making of several great black-and-white 'art' films, local farmers in some extremely poor countries actually amputated their own limbs so as to be paid well for their work as film extras.

Amputation might be the most extreme form of body alteration, but this does open up a very different area of beauty, a much more unique and tribal beauty, which for me involves really interesting people, who challenge our view of beauty and defy our cultural norms. From body-piercers to the tattooed to those who practise body modification, these are people who don't subscribe to the global-village image. Body modification is not for the weak-hearted. It involves a certain degree of sado-masochism and an acceptance that you're going to be stared at for the rest of your life. The more extreme types of transformations are those carried out by 'cat people' – men and women who've had large whiskers implanted through their cheeks, and cat-like tattoos drawn all over their bodies and faces. The effect is quite extraordinary.

In America there is a small East and West Coast trend that involves having living coral horns implanted under the skin of the scalp. These can slowly grow into their own unpredictable shape, and transform an otherwise normal-looking boy or girl into a living demon. This procedure is illegal in most states across the US, but the demand is so high that some tattoo parlours risk prosecution to do it anyway. It cannot be denied that people are getting ever braver and taking more risks when it comes to modifying their bodies.

For some individuals who demand escapism in the way they look and in their 'lifestyle' but cannot find affordable surgery, some shockingly dangerous trends have emerged, especially in the US. To make themselves appear more feminine, some gay transsexual males are seeking alternative ways to change their faces, in an attempt to fulfil their desire for larger female cheekbones and fuller lips. In the States, however, not only are surgeons reluctant to conduct this sort of treatment, but the number of high-grade silicone implants needed makes it astronomically expensive. Instead these transsexual men hold 'pumping parties', at which whole groups inject their faces with industrial silicone without any medical training. This is an incredibly dangerous procedure to carry out, for so many reasons. Whereas the silicone used for breast implants is high-grade and is contained in a protective pocket, industrial silicone is produced exclusively for use in engines, not in the human body. Also it has a different molecular structure that the body cannot cope with, and if this type of silicone isn't contained within a protective covering it can leak to other areas of the body and become attached to vital organs or damage the face. Consequently there are increasing numbers of cases of 'death by industrial silicone' in the US.

These eccentricities do not exclusively belong to male transsexuals or to people who cannot afford a top surgeon. If you visit the website *www.awfulplasticsurgery.com*, one of the names most commonly referred to is a New York society millionairess known as Jocelyn Wildenstein. Personally I love these adventurous people, as it takes a lot of mettle to put oneself 'outside of the norm'. Jocelyn allegedly desired feline eyes and because she could afford the best available surgeon she decided to go for it. This once naturally beautiful woman ended up with cheek, chin and lip implants and also had her eyes reshaped, all because she wanted her ex-husband to notice her. Unfortunately the pictures of her caused such controversy that it proved that although body modification is available to all, it does not necessarily suit all.

It seems we are all taking these steps because we want attention, whether it be for love, admiration or respect. For me, in a strange way, I've chosen to do it because I want to 'fit in', but I know if I achieve this goal, then I will probably find the destination dull, rebel against it, and walk away. I always do.

From my point of view it's been a huge relief to get any surgery out of the way. I feel younger now, and so I hope my facelift will last me fifteen years, by which time I will be realistic and allow myself to age gracefully from then on . . . I think.

In today's society I do feel that women get a raw deal in the grand scheme of things. If we're not an appealing shape we're 'fat'; if we have wrinkles we're 'hags'; if we look good we're 'vain'. It's bad enough that we have fluctuating hormones and infertility to deal with in our lives, but when all this is stacked up alongside the ageing process, it can be very difficult to handle. The journey into old age should be natural and comfortable, but thanks to the critical judgements imposed on us by society, it ain't! As long as women continue to be judged by their appearance, nothing will ever change for the better.

I had lunch with my sister today. She was non-committal about how I looked, but admitted that she wanted her upper eyelids done and that a doctor friend of hers was willing to carry out the procedure for her under a local anaesthetic during a lunch hour. I was horrified. No matter how good her medical friend is, invasive surgery is not a lunchtime procedure; she would need adequate rest and pampering afterwards. My sister has been a nurse in the past and is now a financial manager for the NHS with responsibility for setting up specialized units, such as cancer wards. It took my breath away that she wasn't prepared to invest both time and money in getting the best possible surgeon for the job, or to give herself enough time for her body to recover. This would not be like a casual trip to the dentist. It would involve much greater commitment and is serious enough to warrant considerable thought and proper planning.

MONDAY 22 MARCH 2004

There's a new sensation creeping its way up and across my face. A sense of tightness that spiders up from my neck right into my eyes and scalp, which makes it seem as though I'm standing in a wind tunnel. My eyes feel so tight, almost as if they were being compressed into their sockets. I don't look any different but in comparison to the taut feeling I have from my neck, this tension feels like rubber stretching across the face.

My spirit wants me to focus and write, which is something I have grown to love during these past few days. It has given me a sense of fulfilment like no other, but with my eyes dry and sore it's almost like telling a runner to move while their legs are tied together . . .

TUESDAY 23 MARCH 2004

I take great pride in the fact that I do not smoke or drink, and that my diet consists of fresh fruit and veg for optimum nutrient absorption and maximum detoxing. I've cut down on dairy products, and coffee, tea and fizzy drinks are also banned from my daily menu. Following these crucial dietary guidelines has made a massive improvement to my health, to the extent that my annual battle with the common cold has been reduced from once a year to once every two years.

Here I am living in my world of preventive medicine and enjoying an alternative lifestyle. I take my homeopathic remedies and supplements to prevent illness and encourage mental well-being. I sleep instead of partying and meditate when stressed (or at least I try to). So how can I justify the fact I've just gone and had plastic surgery? For all the effort I've made to try to look after my body in the most natural way possible, I have just taken the most unnatural of routes to deny my age and to hold off the ageing process for a little while longer. Why? In my view I had no option, because despite my commitment to using all manner of alternative, natural remedies and treatments, I knew that I would not be properly able to regain my lost youth any other way. At least I can admit to having this contradictory side of my nature, and I know I'm not unique in how I feel about such things; society is surrounded by contradictions.

Is vanity one of the seven deadly sins? Not exactly, but pride pretty much covers the same territory. Pride, envy, gluttony, lust, anger, avarice and sloth: I'm not doing too badly on all seven as a whole. In the last two months I've practised the lot! Perhaps 'tampering' should become the eighth sin.

The seven sins could have their contrary virtues, of course, such as humility, kindness, abstinence, chastity, patience, liberality and diligence. I'm not doing too badly on those either, except I think that chastity undermines the whole lot. In 2004, preaching chastity is like saying, 'Here's the chocolate bar. It's yours, but don't eat it.'

And thus we're back to square one, the problem facing us all today, which is that because everything is readily available and being flaunted before us, how can we possibly abstain?

WEDNESDAY 24 MARCH 2004

Previously I've mentioned the 'Oh my God, what have I done?' stage, and now I'd like to add a new level to the process which I'm calling the 'I now don't give a damn' stage. It amazes me that my attention has been held so long. It's just one day over a month, which is something of a record for me. Usually my concentration lasts a week, or two paragraphs if I'm writing.

Because my left eye is healing slowly, I'm having to pull hard on the reins. I cannot do photo sessions in case some ambitious scribe decides to latch on to the eye problem and air it in public. The memory of Leslie Ash's public roasting is still fresh in my mind even though it began well over a year ago. At the moment when she needed support, after experiencing an allergic reaction to a treatment on her lips, the media cruelly mocked her, which made me feel sick to my stomach. It was bullying of the worst kind.

My husband, bless him, told me that the eye isn't noticeable, and he is perfectly right as long as I don't dip my head and give that flirtatious Princess Diana look. I'm surprised to discover that I do it far more often than I ever realized. I look perfect until I lower my head and raise my eyes. This, for women, is our prize move: it says 'Help me, I'm truly weak,' when we really mean 'Give me what I want or you die by my words!' I've estimated that I make this move about thirty times a day, and if my eye wasn't playing up I'd probably do it permanently, only ever stopping to take a look in the mirror.

I am bored with the waiting. The world does not stop spinning and I need to get out there and be competitive; after all, that's why I put myself through the rigours of the past month. I want to kick arse for another decade. So let me go forward kicking. They say we have a second childhood as we get older, and if that's true then this second coming won't find *me* being seen and not heard – I'm too damned qualified to lie down in a corner and die!

On the news last night it was announced that the planet Mars once had a 'salty sea'. How undramatic a description is that? 'Salty sea' makes it sound like a river of semen! Orson Welles will be turning in his grave. So is there life on Mars? Is there any element of truth in H. G. Wells's *The War of the Worlds*? I couldn't help thinking that it would be good to hear something a bit more exciting about this much talked-about planet in our solar system.

What will be the legacy of our civilization here on earth, I wonder? Today the valleys of California are filling up with the imperishable breast implants of the deceased first generation of boob-job pioneers. Their implants can't even be destroyed in the crematoriums, let alone in the soil. In a thousand years' time, if there are no video records around to explain our culture, what will future generations think of us?

First it was the caveman who discovered fire and the spear, which was followed by the wheel, then iron, then the mechanics of building bridges, then the steam train, electricity, penicillin, microwave and radiowave communication, the World Wide Web, a 'salty sea on

Mars' – and indestructible silicone implants. Are we going in the right direction?

In the evening I drove to my London home to be ready for my morning appointment with the doctor at Claridge's.

FRIDAY 26 MARCH 2004

I woke up this morning at 4 a.m. My eye was red, which was a first, and it actually looked sore as though the scar had opened slightly. There didn't seem any point in trying to go back to sleep as I had too many things on my mind. Firstly, it was clear that I needed to take some immediate action about this damned eyeball. Secondly, I'd been having trouble with Ealing Borough Council, which was refusing to give me a parking permit despite the fact that I'd lived at my London address for ten years. Tensions were running high, and when you feel this pissed off, sleeping isn't really an option as it just gives your inner gremlins time to play up in your head. Instead I got up and wrote the council a pissy letter, which actually made me feel a lot better.

On top of all this, when I collected the morning papers at 7 a.m. I could see that every tabloid was running a story on Anne Robinson. They showed two photographs of her: one from 2003 in which she looked her age (which I would guess is somewhere in her mid-fifties), and a picture of her today in which she looked about forty. Anyone in the business knows that a combination of good make-up and lighting can take years off you, as can airbrushing, but in this case Anne looked as though she had had the plastic surgery she can afford, which is doubtless the world's best. Though Anne was claiming it was just good make-up, one thing couldn't be denied: she looked bloody fantastic!

It concerns me greatly that there are women out there who are going to clinics that they can just about afford, or even to the cheapest surgeon they can find, believing that, by law, all standards and procedures in the field of cosmetic surgery are the same wherever you go, when that is definitely not the case.

If women like Anne and myself either keep quiet about or deny our efforts to maintain our youth then instead of helping other women find the right sort of treatment, we might possibly be driving them into the hands of unscrupulous money grabbers. I believe we should go public and force an improvement in standards, wherever it is needed. If we unite and stand proud, there might be a chance that we can help avoid a repeat of the trauma suffered by the wife of footballer Colin Hendry, who after 'routine' liposuction was in a coma for weeks, as well as the tragic demise of Olivia Goldsmith, author of *The First Wives Club,* who died of heart failure while under anaesthesia during a facelift. Though her death wasn't caused by the surgery itself, it is important to make clear that such risks exist for every patient undergoing major cosmetic surgery. I believe that we should have a say in how this multi-million pound industry is developing, as it's our money that's helping it to grow. After all, this isn't about star status and wealth; it's about equality and quality for all – everyone deserves the best.

When I arrived at Claridge's with my reddened eye, Dr Olivier de Frahan took one look at me and was very concerned. 'Why didn't you call me?' he asked. He was genuinely amazed that I'd not telephoned for help. To be honest I couldn't see the point. He had been in Paris and I had been in Worcestershire.

'I did tell you about this eye two weeks ago,' I informed him calmly.

'I know, but it has got worse and it should have got better. Did you take your drops? Did you massage?'

'Yes and yes.'

'Well, you're not very good at it,' he replied, but

without heat in his voice. He led me to the window to use the daylight to see more clearly, and I showed him how differently the eye muscles were working on each side by squinting and contracting each eye alternately. This did the trick as he could now see the problem. I'm glad I thought of it because it ploughed a way forward, which I hadn't managed to do two weeks ago. He asked me to flex one side then the other, which made it terribly clear that something was wrong.

'The line of the cut is different under the left eye. It looks broader and deeper,' I said, without sounding in the least bit accusatory.

'No, it's not. I did both eyes exactly the same, the same procedure, so this should not be happening,' he replied. He was greatly sympathetic and studied the skin intensely. 'When do you begin work?'

'I need to start as soon as possible. I've been asked to front a new advertising campaign, but I can't possibly be photographed like this.'

'No. No, you must not.' He paused to think. 'You have to come to Paris. I need to give you cortisone injections, but I want to do it at my office. The internal-muscle scar has gone hard, and you must massage it three times a day like this,' he said, before proceeding to bully the scar into submission as if he was moulding putty. He was far firmer than I had been in the last two weeks and it was slightly painful.

'At night you must stick the area below the eye, up.' This, I thought, will keep Robert entertained for hours, as the doctor was more or less instructing me to impersonate Quasimodo in the nocturnal hours. 'You place tape here, under the left eye. Then you pull it up to here, just for the night times.' And he indicated that the tape should be attached above the middle line of the eye to the side of the upper eyelid.

'Madness!' I thought. It meant that the skin of the lower lid would be pulled up and stuck to the top lid, not unlike the way that a young boy might play with his eyes to achieve a 'scary monster' effect.

'Will I need further surgery?' I asked nervously, dreading an answer in the affirmative.

'No!' he replied, sounding surprised at the suggestion. 'It will return to normal by itself. You have a muscle inflammation that retards the healing process. You can see it; your eye is swollen. But you must massage and I will post you some eye ointment.'

I knew what that was. It's the foul oily stuff I had to put on for a week after the operation. You can't see a thing once it's in, so I'll be forced to play 'blind man's buff' around the house.

He took photographs of my well-practised muscle contortions, to help him decide how to inject the muscles, and we left it that he would call me and make arrangements, though I get the feeling that I'm the one who'll remember to call him.

I left feeling happy that he had acknowledged that there was a problem. At least I knew that I wasn't going to have to live with it for ever and spend the rest of my life trying to cover it up with 'good make-up'.

What really made my day was when I met a girl friend for lunch on Bond Street, a part of London I wouldn't normally be seen in as I consider it a place for airheads who want to burn their money and spend their maturity in poverty. (I'm too penny-pinching for such an illustrious part of London.)

My friend is wealthy beyond guessing, stylish and a successful designer. She wines and dines with supermodels and world megastars, in fact one party she took me to had Paul McCartney in one corner and Salman Rushdie in another. She knows what's good and what's bad, and so it was delightful to hear that she thought my face was the cleverest thing she had ever seen.

'Oh, my God! You look wonderful! That is extraordinary, and to change your hair colour too. How clever!'

She couldn't even see the scars and thought my face was perfect in its 'tightness'. I secretly got the feeling that she would have done the same, but as with all my girl friends she doesn't need it, plus her husband wouldn't tolerate it. This is a common problem for women as it is often the case that a wife will have to go off in secret for her surgery and not tell her husband until some time later because he had always threatened to leave her if she went under the knife. On many occasions the husband will then admit that his wife looks better and he didn't really like her 'saggy boobs' or 'droopy jowls', but hadn't wanted to lose control of his wife's actions or decisions.

SATURDAY 27 MARCH 2004

I'd be taken for a total fool if I revealed that, last night, on the advice of the doctor, I went to sleep with a strip of sticking plaster attached to the skin of the lower eye area, then pulled that up to cover the top eyelid; but that's just what happened My husband laughed. I looked like the result of something that children do with rubber bands, deliberately deforming themselves to shock their parents.

This morning when I awoke, however, my eye was perfect. For some extraordinary reason the skin and the muscles appear to be malleable and can be educated. For the first time in four weeks I believed that the eye could correct itself, and indeed will correct itself given time and copious amounts of sticking tape. Perhaps I won't need to return to Paris, but because I couldn't have a proper look around last time I really fancy going back on my own, which is something I have never done. It is a friendly city and the Parisians seem to be reasonably forgiving of those who haven't quite grasped their language yet.

As the day progressed I could feel the left eye stiffening again. The return to normality had only been temporary this time, and this tightness was definitely an indication that the eye was slipping back into an 'old' habit. Once I bully it into submission again it will go back to how it was this morning. It's up to me to re-educate the muscle until it has a new memory of the shape that it's supposed to be.

TUESDAY 30 MARCH 2004

I take everything back about my assumption that I would have to remind the doctor about my eye appointment, because he phoned just as he said he would. He left a message telling me that he would need me in Paris on Wednesday, Thursday or Friday, while also apologizing for my eye, saying, 'These things can happen; it is scarring of the muscle.'

Good! I can now plan around that. I will go on my own, which should be fun. There are plenty of people I can think of going with but they will want to shop, and I'd rather have a coffee enema than go shopping!

WEDNESDAY 31 MARCH 2004

It was a big day today. I had a lunch appointment with my acting agent Michael Hallett who, at the time when I was deciding whether or not to take the plunge, had been dead against my having surgery. I decided to dress really smartly!

Before that engagement I had a quick photo session for the *Daily Mail*. Telling the photographer I'd just had an eye operation I asked him to watch out for me looking at all funny. He was cool. The photo was fine, but having lost the muscle definition that I liked to have, I felt that I was the size of a house.

As soon as I walked into Michael's office I could tell he was taken aback. I'd dyed my hair really, really red, as far as I could go without reverting back to my crazy-colour days from the 1980s.

'You look fucking wonderful,' he remarked. 'Let's have a closer look!'

Even after I showed him the scars he still thought it was brilliant and nothing more was said about his attempts to try to dissuade me in the first place.

Michael noticed everything he should have. The neck, the eyes, the jaw line and a hair colour that says 'I'm a challenge, a hot redhead who wants to be noticed.' I'd never seen him so focused and interested before. During lunch the subject of 'sex appeal' arose, and I was told that it's a crucial element in the quest to find work. Apparently, people have to want to sleep with you, and I was reliably informed that I'd succeeded in adding that skill to my CV – I've regained my sex appeal! It's about time too; I'm forty-six in seven weeks' time.

Something has recently occurred to me, and it makes me realize how easily we forget a sight when we don't see it in front of us any more. What I'd always hated about ageing was that I could see my face was getting physically longer and growing more 'hangdog'. I couldn't bear it and so I stopped looking in the mirror. It wasn't until last week, when my friend Penny Smith remarked to me 'Your face is so small', that it dawned on me that the dreaded length in my face, the permanent miserable look, has now been removed.

THURSDAY 1 APRIL 2004

Dr Olivier de Frahan was supposed to call me yesterday to confirm a trip to Paris on Friday, but he didn't. I texted him twice, firstly to ask whether the meeting was still going ahead, and secondly to tell him that my eye was responding to the massage and was noticeably improved since last week. I also asked whether it was possible to leave the cortisone injections until he returned to England after Easter. He didn't reply.

I grew bored waiting, and because I'd been left waiting it became an excuse not to write and instead I was lolloping around doing fuck all. It doesn't matter how much money you spend on yourself; fundamentally you're the same person underneath and my capacity for boredom has certainly not been cured by the reduction of my wrinkles. Still, at least my eye is improving. When I don't smile I look fabulous, and when I smile I crease a bit, but I still look better every day and today I could see the definition in my cheekbones returning.

I did my first workout tonight. During those times when I'm in a rut and feeling mentally blocked, as if energy isn't flowing through me, I find that working out is the only way I can lift myself out of it. In fact the exercise often takes me in completely the opposite direction and I stay up all night on a high. As well as going stir crazy at the moment, I've also been putting on some weight due to recent inactivity, and so serious exercise is the only way I can regain my focus. So on went Björk's *Greatest Hits* and I shimmied around the kitchen until the sweat was dripping. It really did the trick. I began to feel human again and, even better, my face didn't go 'twang' and hit my knees!

SATURDAY 10 APRIL 2004

The last two weeks have been difficult beyond description and it has had nothing to do with my plastic surgery. I can only say that the tension in the air was caused by atmospheric changes similar to those that I've heard occur in the German city of Frankfurt during a special time known as the 'season of high pressure', when the weather seems to drive people stark raving mad and the suicide rate triples. Though I haven't felt suicidal, the way I have been feeling is impossible to explain or justify. My life is good, I have no problems or worries other than the frustrations of my own ambitions and I've learned to live with those. But in the last two weeks I've been as ratty as hell and unable to tolerate the company of people, which is unfortunate because there are six billion of them on the planet. I haven't liked myself this last fortnight, not in the least.

Interestingly, Dr Olivier de Frahan called me last Monday (5 April) and left a message in a tense and strangled voice: 'Toyah, I am so sorry not to get back to you. I have such a difficult week, so busy. Please call me and we discuss you coming to Paris.' From the strain in his voice I wondered whether he too had been suffering from the effects of strange atmospheric pressures.

I don't want to go to Paris now. I spent last week waiting in vain for the call to go there and not only did it bugger up my writing plans, but it also frustrated me to the point where I found myself shouting at my mother for mowing the lawn outside my cottage where I was trying to write. What a cow I have become.

One good thing is my eye is responding really well to massage and now looks normal. So I called the doctor and told him that I was fine and I'd wait to see him at the end of the month at Claridge's. He replied, 'But you have big photo-shoot. The cortisone will heal you quicker if I inject the eyelid muscle or the eye will heal correctly anyway in time. This is up to you.'

I decide that I need to write and haven't got time to travel to France. I have a literary agent waiting on my delivering a full manuscript of a children's book, so I want to put my head down and submerge myself in that. Paris isn't necessary.

I spent an hour on the phone last night with a well-known TV actress who was gobsmacked when I told her I'd had surgery. My revelation hit her like a bolt out of the blue. When I told her that I'd written a diary about it she screamed with excitement. All in all she was positive and spent fifteen minutes talking about Anne Robinson and speculating about why she wouldn't come clean about her situation. The fact is that Anne isn't obliged to say anything, and neither am I, but I would feel really uncomfortable denying something that was so glaringly obvious. (Days after I had finished writing this diary entry, however, Anne Robinson went public and confirmed that she had indeed undergone facial cosmetic surgery, as many had suspected. Good for her!)

I talked to my friend about the potential career suicide of publishing such a diary, but like me she thinks the lid should be blown off the 'secrecy and denial' that surround the subject in our business, especially as there are going to be more and more of us who suddenly start to look better as we age. Her last words were, 'Break the back of the taboo, do it [the book] before anyone else does.' To be honest I can't think of anyone else who would want to do it. It would be a brave soul who could bear to be remembered for having a facelift and writing about it. But as I'm thinking about writing a small book on how to tackle the menopause through diet, I may as well cover every taboo going . . .

THURSDAY 15 APRIL 2004

It's fifty-two days and thirteen and a half hours since my operation, and finally I can say that I'm starting to look pretty damned good. My cheekbones are pronounced and rounded, youthful and high, and even though the nose-to-mouth lines were never completely obliterated, the doctor has done a superb job in taking at least ten years of gravitational pull out of them. Could it possibly be that, yes, my skin is getting tighter as time goes by? Hurrah, I say. Furthermore I won't be needing any cortisone injections as my eyes have settled and are close to normal, except for the fact that they are slightly widened and now look fabulous!

Former *Brookside* actress Julie Peasgood interviewed me yesterday and was flabbergasted at the difference. Yet again the change in my hair colour was also regarded as a major improvement to my all-round appearance.

The one downside is feeling as though I'm heavier than I was before. I weighed myself a few days ago and discovered that I was the same weight as when I went to Paris, but unfortunately my body isn't as toned. I am desperate to have a good run or go to a fitness class, but I have to remind myself that two years of onstage aerobics in *Calamity Jane* is what drew my face down to my knees in the first place. My body still needs time to heal and adjust.

Rather than worry about things too much I thought 'Sod it!' I put my favourite CDs on, worked up a good sweat and felt so virtuous afterwards. I pray nothing starts to droop as a result.

For the past six months I have been participating in a course designed to help sufferers of dyslexia and dyspraxia called the Dore Programme. My dyslexia was something I had known about since I was five, but when I was diagnosed with dyspraxia in November 2003 it was both a shock and a revelation. In addition to dealing with the effects of impaired motor co-ordination, dyspraxia sufferers can also have difficulty maintaining attention and concentration. My husband pointed out that the real tell-tale sign for me was that my eyes were never still; they were always moving even when I felt I was focused on a subject. When I was eventually tested with eye scanning, my condition was finally brought to light.

The course I have been on for the last six months is drug free and consists of very simple balance exercises designed to stimulate the cerebellum. I went for an assessment yesterday and I told the practitioner about the surgery I'd had, describing how for about a week after the operation it had felt as though I'd had a stroke, and that all my spelling was backwards. She told me that this was the result of stopping the exercises and that once I resumed the treatment it would sort itself out.

When she did her assessment of my progress the scan revealed my eyes had become normal and my balance test had improved by 90 per cent. I was informed that it usually took two years to achieve this level of progress, sometimes longer, and that I would be at peak levels within six to eighteen weeks. This really surprised me as immediately after the operation I felt I'd regressed so badly that it would take a least a year to get back to any 'normality'.

The odd thing is that although I hadn't restarted the exercises since my operation, my brain patterns had continued to improve. Since the surgery I've written 70,000 words for this project and a further 50,000 of a children's novel, which is a miracle in itself because my dyslexia has been really bad in the past. The course has somehow enhanced my focus and attention; in the last month alone I've written more than I've ever managed in a year. I also feel that the quality of my writing has improved immeasurably, which is a fantastic achievement for me.

There's no doubt that this is a year in which I'm getting my act in order. I'm in the middle of a life audit and am laying foundations for the rest of my working life, which I want to be as lengthy as possible. Time, science and attitudes have progressed so much since I was a child that people are now able to deal with problems they thought they'd be stuck with for life. For example, I'm still dyslexic but I'm somehow more capable, and writing is no longer the immense enemy it was in the past.

Next I intend to learn about computers. I have a dream of writing in a faraway country and e-mailing my work to different continents across the globe. Funnily enough, I feel that since I've had plastic surgery I am ready to become anonymous and walk away from the celebrity culture that has replaced true talent and real achievement in today's society. It might be a fleeting notion, but I have regained my confidence to the extent that I no longer crave outside attention. It's a confidence

I've never had before. The only job I've ever known is to act and entertain, but somehow my priorities have shifted, and I feel certain I can work without the need for constant approval.

TUESDAY 20 APRIL 2004

The honeymoon period is *so* over. I'm ready to divorce my convalescence and elope with the first job offer, which could be with Timmy Mallet for all I care. Now I need a life.

The last two weeks have been unusually horrible. The weather has been shite and cast its dullness on every aspect of life. But the year seems to be perking up again. I suppose one must take solace in the fact that if you're feeling so bad about everything at least sixty million others are probably in a similar state.

Two weeks ago I was stricken by plain and simple madness, which thankfully disappeared as soon as the full moon buggered off, and over the last weekend I was indescribably down. When Robert is away I never feel like turning cartwheels in the sand, but I do usually get on with life. So I decided to phone most of my work colleagues from *Calamity Jane* to catch up with their lives, but not one of them called me back, which made me even more blue. Fortunately I had better luck with all my old mates from *I'm A Celebrity, Get Me Out Of Here!* All of them returned my calls and they really cheered me up. Danniella Westbrook, Chris Bisson and Sîan Lloyd got back to me and we spent hours chatting on the phone. Only Danniella had known about my trip to Paris and she was dead excited for me.

I am through the two-month barrier now and am so ready to get on with things. Over the next two weeks I've got five photo sessions and numerous TV appearances, so I'll be waiting to see if anyone notices anything different about me. I'll be really narked if they don't.

I've grown so used to my 'new' face that I've no memory of how it was before, though sometimes when I look in the mirror I'm not even sure if I look any different. As all my swelling reduces then wrinkles reappear and I feel I need Botox around my eyes, even though the doctor has said I never will again. Compared to Anne Robinson, who looks twenty years younger all of a sudden, I just look firm and fresh. It seems to me that Anne has not only had a lift but also a skin peel. Admittedly in the pictures I saw of her she was under studio lights, which always add lustre. The test for me will come when I'm next in a studio, because before the op not even a million lights could iron out the droop under my eyes. Perhaps the proof of the pudding lies in going back to work and seeing if the changes are substantial on camera.

Now I'm over the worst of things I want to get my stomach done. I have a relatively flat tum, in fact I am toned and have the same waist size I had thirty years ago, but surgery these days can give you the chance to expose your midriff with pride again. Also I want breast reduction, because to me having smaller breasts makes a woman look younger. However, this is the one operation my husband will not let me have. As far as he is concerned, big is beautiful in the boob department. It seems that two months after the op, all the hassle is beginning to fade, and I'm now able to reconsider my feelings about going through more surgery. Perhaps it's like childbirth, when once the pain is forgotten you want to do it all over again.

FRIDAY 23 APRIL 2004

Back in London this morning, I walked down Savile Row for the first time in almost a decade. It is not a street or district that I frequent. The last time I was there I was escorting the Page Three model Sam Fox to my production office for British:American Films, which was located at the end of the street. Throughout the 1990s I dabbled in film and TV production, and on that day Sam was attending the launch of the company.

As she teetered on tiny, heel-elevated feet towards my office, all around us traffic was screeching to a halt and men of all shapes and sizes, all ages and professions, were making complete idiots of themselves, the way cats do when they get a whiff of catnip. These men lost all self-control and instead of inflating their manly chests they turned into blubbering jellies. Sam loved it, but she was more than used to this sort of reaction. As for me I was shocked that, while in her presence, I'd simply faded into the background and become completely invisible, a blot on the landscape, a shadow blocking the view. The fame that my films, records and TV career had created simply wasn't part of the equation that day; it was pure flesh that this broad social spectrum of men wanted, dusted with a bit of notoriety and a cheeky Barbara Windsor-type smile. Despite the fact that I was smart, attractive, well turned out and recognizable, I just wasn't 'lustworthy'. It's not surprising that the American porn industry has a higher economic turnover in Hollywood than that produced by the blockbuster films we all know. Sam wasn't part of any porn industry, of course, but her career cleverly gave the illusion that she was 'up for anything', and what a reaction she had on the opposite sex because of it. Fortunately I only felt worthless for a day or two afterwards.

Today I was walking down Savile Row to visit a producer friend. I was wearing a tight black T-shirt, black trousers and trainers, my face was fully made up for a photo session later in the day, and my hair was long, red and flowing. I felt really 'up' about life, despite being a little over my ideal weight through lack of training during my recovery, and dwelling on the fact that the excess weight had gone to my boobs (which is something I hate). However, traversing the street on this occasion, I found that the traffic was screeching to a halt, and some cars were even reversing back towards me, while a chorus of wolf whistles hung in the air. It was me that was getting this attention! One van reversed back down the street, and looking out of the window were two boys, gawping open-mouthed at me.

'You're off the telly, aren't you?'

'Yep!' I say.

'Don't you present *Big Brother*?'

The thought that they had mistaken me for Davina McCall had me in fits of laughter, especially as I'm at least ten years older than her and about a foot smaller. But the wolf whistles kept coming and so did the mistaken identities: from Davina to Kirsty Gallacher the Sky Sports TV presenter! I'd never been whistled at in the street before, and though I wasn't sure whether this should have worried me, I found I liked it. It reminded me of what it was like to exert some invisible power over the opposite sex.

What did become clear to me was that it wasn't just my chest that had provoked this reaction, but the changes in my face had also played a part. Sam Fox has a pixie-shaped face with a slightly pointed chin that is neither too assertive nor too masculine, and following my surgery I now have a similar shape. To me it signals an irresistible youthful innocence that's hugely appealing to the opposite sex, and which I hope will last.

WEDNESDAY 28 APRIL 2004

Damn! Damn! Damn! I am an arse! I'd returned home to Worcestershire last night to be ready for a visit from a *Sunday Times* journalist who was due to interview me about my garden. She was clearly good at her job because she asked about everything *but* the garden, including how often I was at home and how many other properties I owned. When we walked around the garden together she asked me absolutely nothing about it. Instead I was quizzed about such things as 'Have you had planning permission for this and that?' – which struck me as rather stupid as it is a period property where everything is more than a hundred years old. The subject of the interview was supposed to be my gardening technique, but all the time she was examining my face and my clothes. Some journalists have the ability to make you feel as though you've just been 'frisked' in their company, and despite being female she had the same invasive quality as a predatory male. I still found her company an enjoyable challenge, however, and we continued talking for quite some time.

She also wanted to know about the house, the hint of cynicism in her voice suggesting that I knew nothing about period property, so I gave her a tour. In my study was a brand-new computer, which Robert had brought back from America for me, and because I was so enamoured of its abilities, I showed it to her. As I turned it on, the first thing that came up on screen was a whole page of post-op photos of me that Robert had down-loaded at my request. AARRGGHH! I couldn't get them off the screen quick enough! I wasn't sure whether she'd noticed as she'd been nosing around my desk at the time, but talk about divine comic timing.

THURSDAY 29 APRIL 2004

The lady who runs my local Holland and Barrett store in Worcestershire has a fabulous way with words and I've spent quite a bit of time with her researching herbs and natural remedies for various interviews and after-dinner speeches. Today I went in for information on red clover, which is a wild plant that's particularly good for women going through menopause because it's high in natural oestrogens. I've been asked to become the face of a product line that uses red clover and I wanted to know if it had received any bad press lately, which it hadn't. While I was reading through the written material available in the shop, the assistant said to me, 'My, you've lost weight. Your whole face shape has changed.' She had seen a lot of me in the last few months as I'd also dropped by when my face was fully swollen. Throughout that period she kept telling me how well I looked, but she couldn't put her finger on why. Today she'd put it down to weight loss.

My face is changing daily now as the swellings are all diminishing. I have cheekbones and the scars around the ears are almost invisible. I would like some Botox under the eyes because without the added swelling the wrinkles are still there, albeit just a little, though they're 90 per cent better than before, and so I'm certain that just a drop of Botox could erase them totally.

TUESDAY 4 MAY 2004

Today I decided it was time to visit my Botox man, Dr Patrick Bowler, for the first time since my op. His first reaction was to comment on how incredible I looked, and he was most impressed with my surgeon's work. At my request he applied Botox around the lower eye area, and to my immense relief completely eradicated the remaining lines.

MONDAY 15 MAY 2004

Last night I had dinner with the artist P. J. Crook. A fine woman and a brilliant artist, she is someone I would categorize as a feminist icon. Today she e-mailed me to say how wonderful I was looking and by return I confessed the reasons why. This was a chance for me to test the water with the intellectual glitterati, even though P. J. is a hundred times more human than any great thinker I've ever met. Her response was immediate and casual: 'Oh, really? Good for you. I know a lot of people who've done the same.' It transpired that her art dealer in New York had just had a facelift, as had another of her dealers in Paris.

I was expecting harsh criticism for being egotistical and weak, but instead I got honesty and praise. It appears that in the feminist world reclaiming your features is an act of self-expression and strength, which I was pleased to discover. It's obvious that it's rife throughout the world. In fact I'm sure many of the people who criticize plastic surgery have all had it done too. It's like the way that no one owns up to shopping in Poundstretcher, but we all do.

P. J. also added in her e-mail that having a facelift must be the most liberating step a woman can take in order to reclaim her working identity, and reinvent herself at the peak of her prowess. In full agreement with what she had said, I picked up a Sunday magazine from a tabloid today and discovered there were no fewer than five references to plastic surgery made in it, all about women under the age of thirty.

* * *

THURSDAY 9 SEPTEMBER 2004

One month after the operation I looked good, but now it is just over six months since I was in Paris and I look fabulous. My face has virtually returned to what I'd describe as a 'normal' appearance. All the swelling has gone, which is just as it should be at this stage in the process. My scars have settled into the contours of my face so well that they are now invisible. I look natural, but toned, and a hundred times better than I did before the operation. I'd say the treatment has easily taken ten years off me, but by far the greatest improvement comes from within. Confidence now radiates from me and for the first time in ten years I notice that men are looking at me in a positive way. I experience some flirting, and I find that more of an effort is being made to cross a room at a party to talk to me, and I even get the odd wolf-whistle. In recent times I had learned to live without this kind of attention without too much difficulty, or so I believed, but once it had returned I realized that receiving flattery from the opposite sex is an essential part of being a woman. Perhaps it may soften my personality. I sometimes feel like Boudicca confronting the Romans in a bombastic and warlike fashion, but now I might learn the delicate and prosperous art of flattering the opposite sex rather than bulldozing my way through the forest of male egos like some contractor destroying a Brazilian rainforest. Miracles can happen!

My face has full sensation and there are no adverse effects to note, in fact there is nothing negative to report. Apart from the occasional worrying setback about my eyes, the last six months have been the happiest of my life. I feel a massive release from having taken the step of going ahead with the op, and having come through it without any complications, and now I am revelling in a newfound confidence. It has all gone so smoothly, with the daily comments of 'You look so well' still pouring in, that I have nothing to complain about. Except one thing.

In the past six months I have tried to achieve a better me, an improved me. I have been through an extreme reinvention in the hope it will improve my career prospects. It's not just the operation, though, because throughout my recuperation I've been writing two books as well as studying a wide range of subjects from art to scriptwriting, using the recovery time for a spot of education, which is the kind of stuff I missed out on in the punk-rock years. Additionally I've been having meetings with top producers and continuing my dyslexia course, the Dore Programme, all of which have been hugely successful. Looking back it has been a period of conscious rejuvenation, a positive sabbatical.

As well as the facelift, which is the most extreme thing I have ever done in my life, in the last few months I have also just about managed to maintain a healthy diet – no alcohol, no dairy products, more fruit and veg – and taken as much exercise as I can without damaging the work on my face. The doctor advised me not to over-exert myself for a period of twelve months, which I thought was perhaps a little over-cautious, but I accept that I do still have to avoid high blood pressure in case I pull or stress any of the internal work.

I feel in peak condition both physically and mentally. In fact it's the best I've felt about myself in over a decade. My confidence is overflowing and I've adopted a definite attitude of walking around holding two fingers up to the world, daring it to criticize me about my outward appearance. The plain truth is that for a young-minded forty-six-year-old I'm not in bad nick.

Then I walked into the newsagent and saw the front cover of the *Daily Mail* featuring Carol Vorderman, the TV presenter, a similar age to myself, dressed in a white evening dress at a top awards function. She looked so stunning I couldn't help but think, 'What is the point? How can anyone compete with that?' What the picture conveyed was a supernatural beauty. Though Carol doesn't look at all tampered with, and I'm not suggesting she is, her stunning appearance does beg the question, 'If we were all worth £19 million could we all look that good?' I've just gone to hell and back just to look decent, but to look as good as Ms Vorderman I reckon I'd have to have leg extensions, a skin transplant and serious stem-cell surgery to improve my brain beyond its present capacity. In fact I'm not sure that even if I had infinite wealth and enough time on my hands I could look that good!

For most of us, such perfection doesn't fall into our laps. Women from Jane Fonda to Caprice have all gone on record saying it's a 'lifestyle' and a full-time commitment in which you get up at dawn, work out till dusk, eat one lettuce leaf and ignore the hunger pains. It isn't natural to be this perfect and of course this perfection doesn't come naturally. Even if you are blessed with great bones and forgiving genes, you still need the money and the time to go to the gym, see your yoga guru, then your personal trainer, then the masseur, and then you need to find an extra two hours for your daily facial. This is not normal; the majority of us have to spend our days working, and so we don't have the luxury of time on our hands. As for me, I want to work; the thought of lying in a beautician's salon for two hours every day doesn't interest me. In fact it isn't like real life – it's factory farming for glamour.

I can't keep up with this ever-constant race towards perfection. It's running away with itself. I think there should be a law that only allows people to become so beautiful, after which time they can pay a 'beauty tax' to fund us short gremlins and help us to improve at a faster rate. What are we supposed to do? How are we ever to feel satisfied about ourselves if the standards are set at unrealistic, superhuman levels? It makes me despair. I would need a stylist, a personal trainer, a hairdresser, a make-up artist and a plastic surgeon on a lifetime retainer, as well as a permanent colonic irrigation tube up my jacksie just to keep up with the competition. Looking that good costs a fortune, and even after all that there are some people who still don't quite hit the mark, either their skin is too orange or their husband is a hundred times more beautiful than they are. Everyone on the telly is becoming too good-looking and beyond our reach. We need to see more 'average-looking somethings' to make us feel good about ourselves.

My morning has been quite extraordinary, so bizarre in fact that I'm surprised at myself for that last section of whinging. What I witnessed this morning should have taught me better.

I was at the Queen Elizabeth Hospital in Birmingham, opening a new bone-marrow treatment unit. It was one of those times where you saw the miracle of mankind. Lining the corridors were cancer sufferers alongside those who were fortunate enough to be in remission. Their faces were full of light and hope, exuding positive thinking and a lust for life. All uniquely individual, they were the most beautiful people I had ever seen. In this exceptional environment you saw the human being not the image, and the sight of them touched my heart.

After I cut the ribbon I found myself talking to a man of about fifty-five with bone cancer who had had aggressive chemotherapy two days previously and his stem-cell implant the day before, administered by a drip into his arm. Consequently the effect of the treatment meant his immune system would fail in the next twenty-four hours, leaving him so frail and vulnerable that he has to be shut in a sterile room for his own safety for anything up to four weeks to avoid picking up an infection. Even a cold could kill him at that stage. Meeting me was his last outing, his small 'going into the sterile room' party. Together we sat and scoffed cakes that the nurses had set out in the ward lounge. He told me that in a few hours time he would not be feeling well enough to eat, but that in a few weeks his body would start to fight back. The next four weeks would be very hard for him as he loved his outdoor pursuits, and because he didn't like reading he couldn't imagine how he'd keep his sanity in his individual sterile room all alone.

I promised him a strip-o-gram, which he thought was a splendid idea as long as she was blonde. He showed no self-pity or fear, and was completely accepting of his condition and very much existing in the moment and enjoying each extra day he had.

Being among such courageous people I felt terrible guilt. Here was this man who was fighting to get out of hospital, sitting next to someone who, for purely cosmetic reasons, had paid to be put into one. The bitter irony of the situation certainly wasn't lost on me.

SUNDAY 12 SEPTEMBER 2004

It's Sunday. I have a rule that I try and keep, which is to wake up in my own bed on a Sunday morning. That's not to say that I wake in a stranger's bed every other day, of course not. It's simply that my work takes me away from home for most of the week. The thought of the view out of my bedroom window of a forest of verdant branches and the river flowing at the foot of the garden keeps me sane through the long night drives to venues far afield.

My Sunday routine consists of waking at around 6 a.m. and going to my study to write until the newsagent opens. Then I get an assortment of papers and retire to the bath for anything up to four hours. One of this morning's magazine supplements carried a feature on Danniella Westbrook. I noticed in the second paragraph it mentioned her age, which struck me as odd as she was only a baby. I searched through the rest of the magazine and found a feature on Jude Law, which referred to the acting roles he'd had as a child. I thought it would have been appropriate to mention his age somewhere in the article, but it didn't. There was also a list of all the women in his life, past and present, including all their ages. In a piece about Patsy Kensit her age was featured before any other detail about her life. So I went to other stories about normal everyday people who were featured in the magazine, and lo and behold the ages of all the women were featured, but the men's weren't. Out of interest I looked at who'd written which article: a man was responsible for the Danniella piece and a woman for the Jude feature; a woman had written the Patsy article, however, and so I wondered if the sub-editor had added the ages, and whether he happened to be male.

I feel that by even raising such a query I might appear to be waging a war on male opinion and judgement, but this really isn't the case. I'm just being honest. It can't be denied that all our views have been conditioned or influenced by fashion, politics and religion, advertising and marketing, and consequently ageism needs to be addressed, particularly in view of the fact that people (in the western world at least) are expected to live several years longer these days.

Women are natural creatures of reinvention. We are unique in that we have defined stages in our lives from childhood to womanhood and on to motherhood to menopause and then old age. The menopausal years, when we shed the skin of fertility to grow an aura of wisdom, are what give us our uniqueness. There is nothing wrong in being the 'wise woman'. Why should there be? Where is the threat in being the fount of knowledge in the family? I strongly believe that the world should not undermine this attribute; we should not belittle it by leading young women to believe that the inevitable approach to a more mature age is akin to a social disease. As we celebrate the issue of 'diversity' in many other areas of society and humankind, we should also embrace the diversity of age.

Looking old, thinking old, being old, being perceived as old, are all very contrasting situations with different connotations. Old age is an attitude as much as a physical condition, and so we have the right and ability to re-evaluate exactly what old age truly is, in order to make it a more positive experience. It is the choice of the individual to do something about it for themselves. The outside world has no reason to heap pressure upon the natural anxieties that this state of ageing brings; we should all be pointing out that it is a privilege to be here and a privilege to age.

AFTERWORD

THE FACE TELLS THE WORLD WHO WE ARE. It is the first thing we observe when we note a person's race, their age and whether we are attracted to them or not. There are more prejudices surrounding the face than any other part of the human body. Even pets are chosen based on their cute faces and endearing expressions. Close runners-up behind the face for body-part prejudice are breasts, the waist and then the penis. We are all aware of and insecure about the lot, hence the existence of a billion-dollar cosmetic surgery industry.

I'm a lucky person. I've never had much to lose and now that I've regained a little of what I've lost, I fully realize how much it meant to me. But what about the legendary beauties whose whole life revolves around their outward appearance? How is it for them when their looks fade? As they're perceived as the 'goods' in the business side of celebrity, when they start to age many are seen as lost merchandising potential and viewed as a dwindling investment. No matter how talented they are, they will never be forgiven for succumbing to what is only natural. It's worth considering that there have been so few brilliant beauties who have been given the chance to develop their careers as they get older and become legendary character actresses such as Bette Davis. It is hard to grow old in the glare of the spotlight and under the scrutiny of so many critics. Though I believe the human race is capable of great kindness, we seem unable to express it much in the world of show business.

It seems that beauty has become the weapon by which the enemy defines us. Whether we inhabit the world of celebrity or are members of ordinary society, how do we combat this attitude? Do we show indignant indifference? Do we remonstrate that we don't give a damn about what the editors, stylists and trendsetters tell us? Should we be insisting that they send the fourteen-year-old models who grace their pages back to school, and wake up these journalists to the fact that people aged forty-five and above are now in the majority? With our heads full of knowledge and experience, the nest is empty, our purses are full and our time is our own – thus, our lives and our quest for self-expression can truly begin.

It's time that middle age was rightfully recognized as 'sexy', otherwise we should simply close our collective purse and shut the beauty industry down, thereby causing the biggest shoppers' revolution since aerosol cans were blacklisted and left languishing on supermarket shelves. Make middle age sexy or we walk! I don't want to dress in clothes sold off the backs of fourteen-year-olds: I want designs that reflect a life of achievement; I want to adorn myself in metaphoric pert, erect-nippled, flat-bellied, voluptuous pride now. Only images of an uncommon, outstanding youthful beauty make the pages of the billion-dollar magazine-publishing industry. Yet if we were to remove everyone from this planet aged thirty and over, the heart of the world would stop beating. Approximately 50 per cent of the world's population is over fifty years old, and 50 per cent of women are aged forty-five or more. We are living longer and so we need to extend our quality of life. There is no choice in this world of image but to make middle and old age sexy.

Until society's attitude changes, though, the taboos must remain. I have girl friends who've had minor procedures from Botox to peels and some who've had major invasive procedures from brow lifts to neck lifts, and their spouses don't even know because they're too afraid to tell them. Surgery makes some people queasy, perhaps none more so than men. Have men created the culture of prejudice against surgery alongside the anti-ageing culture, thereby demanding that women must look good at all times yet making surgery socially unacceptable? Or have women helped to create a world that judges others by their looks alone? Because we're unable to compete with the perfections of those whose beauty is flaunted from the pages of glossy magazines or on the big screen, when their looks inevitably fade we stand up and cheer in the belief that they've come to know how we feel here in our ordinary 'standard-size land'. Whatever our views, the most important thing is that we have the power to change attitudes, so let's do it!

* * *

It is now twelve months since my op. Without any shadow of a doubt my life has changed completely. In addition to the fact that the surgery has physically altered my 'outer shell' for the better, significant positive changes have also occurred within. My mind, personality and psyche are totally different; I now have an inner peace and confidence, the value of which I cannot even begin to put a price on.

Before the op I was a woman whose personal make-up consisted of 60 per cent anxiety. I worried about everything, and consequently worked myself into a state of exhaustion because I lived in constant fear of time running out. What has changed this attitude? Why has this been the best therapy I could have undergone? There are two reasons: as well as the physical benefits derived from the surgery itself, of equal importance was the fact that I followed my instincts and was prepared to accept the risk of surgery. It wasn't a decision to be taken lightly and required a tremendous leap of faith to set the wheels in motion. My determination paid off and has transformed my life, encouraging me to have faith in myself and my decision-making.

Professionally, I've also started to experience a change in fortunes. The quality of work I'm being offered is of an increasingly high calibre and I'm meeting New York movie directors and Los Angeles film producers. In summer 2004 I had an appointment to see a top director who was casting a particular role in his new movie. The meeting went very well and I was offered the part on the spot. As I was saying my goodbyes, the director took me aside and said, 'You are looking stunning!' I didn't know if he was aware I'd had surgery or whether he even cared either way, but it struck me as interesting that he was compelled to offer me such a compliment. I was delighted!

Why have these doors started to open? The answer, I think, is that as well as looking better on the outside, my newfound confidence has given me a more chilled-out, cool and happy aura, which is definitely rubbing off on those around me. I feel as if I've reclaimed myself, and salvaged my being from some murky dark pool of existence in which I'd been languishing for so long. When performing on stage, whether in rock concerts or in the theatre, I now feel my face matches my naturally hyperactive energy, and I'm proud to be such a good advert for middle age. If the spirit is willing and the body is still capable, why grow up?

Another consequence of my decision to have surgery has been the effect that my transformation has had on men. Though I'd become tired of growing ever more invisible in the eyes of the opposite sex, this issue certainly hadn't been a motivating factor in my decision to opt for a facelift. Since making a full recovery from the treatment, however, I've been surprised and thrilled by the positive reaction I've been getting from men wherever I go. Whether it's an acknowledgement of my enhanced physical appearance or a response to the renewed self-belief that I've been exuding, my cloak of invisibility has lifted and I'm back in vision again.

Looking back over the past year I've been so lucky to have had my husband Robert providing unswerving support from day one. Not only did he have the stomach to back my decision, but he was at my side throughout my recovery. He has always trusted my judgement and was well aware of the risks I was taking. If he ever had the urge to try to stop me, he certainly never expressed it, and from the moment we were reunited in the recovery room in Paris, he assured me I had done the right thing. To him it was evident that the doctor's judgement on how far to improve me was 100 per cent right.

Robert hasn't lost his old wife, he's simply regained the spirited soul whom he married nineteen years ago and is openly proud of the effort I put in to finding the right surgeon and choosing the most appropriate procedure.

When considering whether I would follow this path again, the answer would have to be 'yes'. We shouldn't feel pressured into hiding the results of our surgery; there is no shame in wanting to show the world your true face, who you feel you truly are and how you should really look. For some people their body or physical appearance is more like a prison, and so if surgery can unlock the door and set them free, why not try it? In the modern age reinvention is key. Whether you choose to take the surgical route or improve yourself through education, dieting, detoxing, fitness classes, changing hairstyle or clothes, I've learned it's important to focus on what you want from life, and that if you want something, then go for it.

My journey now complete, I no longer feel a victim of the ageing process and I am more secure in my workplace. The lifelong burden of my tired eyes has been lifted and my face has ceased to wear a permanent expression of stress and exhaustion. I'm fit, healthy and full of confidence – life has never been better.

APPENDIX:
THINKING ABOUT
A FACELIFT?

Cosmetic surgery – a brief overview

'Cosmetic surgery' is the name given to surgical procedures that are intended to restore or improve a person's appearance. It is also sometimes called 'plastic surgery', not because what we think of as plastics are used in its procedures (although silicone plastics have been used in cosmetic surgery for thirty-five years or more), but because the word 'plastic' comes from Greek *plastikos*, from the verb *plassein* meaning 'to mould' or 'form'. Thus a plastic surgeon is someone who 'moulds' tissue to achieve a different appearance, either to repair damage caused by injury, or to achieve an improved look for cosmetic reasons ('aesthetic plastic surgery'). Much plastic surgery in this country is performed to obviate or diminish the effects of, say, injuries received in a fire or a road accident, or to correct physical abnormalities such as large and disfiguring birthmarks.

As previously mentioned, the father of modern plastic surgery was the great New Zealand surgeon Sir Harold Gillies (1882–1960), whose book *Plastic Surgery of the Face*, published in 1920, established the procedure as a recognized branch of medicine. Gillies worked in Britain during the Second World War, as did his most eminent pupil, Sir Archibald MacIndoe (1900–60), another New Zealander, who became famous for his work during that war in remodelling the limbs and faces of injured airmen. Since much of his work was ground-breaking and even experimental, his subjects became known as 'MacIndoe's guinea pigs'.

The six decades since the end of the Second World War have seen not only many advances in cosmetic surgery, but also an increase in both its practitioners and those wishing to undergo one or more of the procedures offered. Greater demand and availability have also led to a comparative fall in prices, although obviously the more complicated the surgery, the greater the cost; similarly, work undertaken by the top practitioners and at the leading institutions will always incur higher prices. Some cosmetic surgery is performed under the auspices of the National Health Service, but this is more usually to correct the effects of injuries or abnormalities, so in practice most such operations are undertaken privately.

There are many different procedures that come under the general heading of 'cosmetic surgery', among the commonest being breast enhancement (or, sometimes, reduction or reshaping), 'tummy tucks', techniques like liposuction to reduce body fat, nose, chin and jaw reshaping, removal of moles and other blemishes, and facelifts. For obvious reasons, this appendix concentrates upon the latter, but anyone wanting information about other procedures will find a list of useful addresses on pages 222–4.

Finally, the argument that people only undergo cosmetic surgery for reasons of vanity is not a strong one. Quite apart from those who have such surgery in order to correct congenital abnormalities, such as a cleft lip, or the effects of injury, like scarring from burns, there are thousands who have cosmetic surgery in order to improve their view of themselves (and thus their self-confidence); vain people generally wish to improve other people's view of them.

What is a facelift?

Put simply, surgery to correct the effects upon the face of time, gravity, skin damage from exposure to the sun, and so on. A facelift – properly, 'rhytidoplasty' or a 'rhytidectomy' – won't make you younger, but it will lessen or remove some of the most visible results of growing older, such as sagging skin, wrinkles and creases, and folds of skin around the neck. There seems, at least anecdotally, to be a general agreement among people who have had facelifts that they look, as a result, at least ten years younger.

What is involved?

The procedure loosely divides into the full facelift, and various 'mini-lifts'. In the former, an incision is usually made in the area of the temple just behind the hairline and continued downwards on both sides of the face just in front of the ear and then beneath the earlobe into the hairline behind the ear. Mini-lifts may be something as simple as an incision under the chin to remove excess fat there, or a 'brow lift', which improves the look of the forehead by lessening the effects of frown lines, wrinkles, drooping eyebrows, and so on, but without going as far as a full facelift; similarly, slackening of the skin of the jaw may be improved by employing incisions just behind the ear. Not everything requires surgery: some skin blemishes can be removed or diminished by the use of lasers, for instance, and other procedures include courses of Botox injections to remove wrinkles. Deciding on what technique to choose is a matter first of all for you, and then for the advice of a qualified and experienced plastic surgeon (see later). Nevertheless, some of the organizations listed on pages 222–4 can provide you with information about different options and techniques, which may help you to form a decision. What you decide upon is obviously a matter for careful consideration, so it is only sensible to find out as much as you can before you make a decision – do not be embarrassed to ask questions, and do not opt for anything until you are absolutely sure in your mind that your decision is the correct one. In some cases, surgeons may recommend a patient for counselling or a psychological assessment before any decision is taken.

Do I have to wait until I'm old?

Most cosmetic surgery is performed on people aged from their forties to their sixties, but it can be successful with older people, and increasingly nowadays people in their thirties, or even their late twenties, are opting for mini-lifts to correct what they see as minor problems with their appearance. For anyone whose livelihood depends upon their appearance – models and actors and actresses, for instance – a mini-lift might well prove beneficial. Again, disinterested advice from a properly qualified practitioner is essential.

How do I find a 'properly qualified practitioner'?

It is a worrying thought that, in this country (and, indeed, much of the EU) anyone with a licence to practise medicine may call themselves a cosmetic surgeon, whether or not they have any training in surgery, let alone plastic surgery. Indeed, there have recently been a number of cases reported of people practising as cosmetic surgeons despite their having had no specialist training. Always check, therefore, that the person you have in mind is registered with the General Medical Council (GMC; see page 222 for address) and that he or she is a qualified surgeon (in which case 'MRCS' or 'FRCS' – Member or Fellow of the Royal College of Surgeons – should appear after the name); bear in mind, though, that a qualified surgeon may not have any training in cosmetic surgery. There are, however, two professional associations whose members will have had proper training in cosmetic surgery: the British Association of Plastic Surgeons (BAPS) and the British Association of Aesthetic Plastic Surgeons (BAAPS; contact details for both are on page 222), and it is obviously a good idea to check out any surgeon with these; similarly, a surgeon registered with the GMC may give his or her membership of one of these bodies among the details lodged with the GMC. Remember, though, that there is currently no legal requirement for a cosmetic surgeon to be a member of either body. At the time of writing, the British government announced the introduction of new legislation to regulate the cosmetic-surgery industry in an attempt to give more protection to patients. Specific details have yet to be released, but updates posted on the Healthcare Commission website (see page 223) should be monitored in the mean time. Finally, you may hear of a surgeon, hospital or clinic from a friend who has undergone cosmetic surgery and been pleased not only with the result, but with the advice given and the standards of pre- and post-operative care. Obviously, a word-of-mouth recommendation from someone you trust (and the success of whose surgery you can judge for yourself) is very valuable, although you should still follow the checks outlined above.

What next?

Having decided upon a surgeon or hospital, you should then have a consultation to discuss with the surgeon who will perform the procedure both what you should opt for, and what will be involved (including, of course, the cost). Many offer a free first consultation, and you should take advantage of this to ask any and all questions that occur to you. Do not let yourself be dazzled by promises of immediate and brilliant results; concentrate instead on finding out, first, what type of facelift you should have, and second, what will be involved. Take the opportunity, too, to make some general observations: is the place maintained to a high standard? Do the nursing and other staff seem competent and pleasant? Have you been given all the information you want? Are you certain that there are no hidden charges above and beyond the price you have been quoted? Above all, do you have confidence in the surgeon who will perform your own facelift?

Blood tests

Before facelift surgery can proceed, you need to have certain blood tests to establish such details as your blood type, HIV status, haemoglobin count, hormonal balance and whether your body contains adequate vitamins and minerals to cope with such a major operation. You also need to have an electrocardiogram (ECG) to enable the anaesthetist to check your heart-rate and ascertain that you are healthy enough to proceed with surgery. Your surgeon will either arrange these tests for you, or give you recommendations and details about which private clinics to contact. The estimated cost of these tests is between £200 and £350, but different establishments will vary.

How much?

The cost of cosmetic surgery varies considerably, since the overall charges depend upon what procedure you opt for and, to a certain extent, upon whom you engage to perform the surgery and, perhaps, where you have it done. According to a recent survey in *The Times* newspaper (January 2005), the cost of facelift surgery varies from £650 to £7,860, but bear in mind that VAT will add to that. There may also be additional charges for post-operative care, medication and so on, so it is only sensible to find out everything you can about charges before agreeing to surgery, and to try to work to a budget. Finally, *The Times* warns its readers about some so-called 'free consultations' – some surgeons or organizations will charge you for the consultation if you decide not to go ahead with surgery. Again, find out beforehand and make sure you are provided with a note of any charges in writing – a 'free consultation' should be just that: free.

Is it dangerous?

All surgery – even the simple lancing of a boil – carries some degree of risk. Given a well-trained and experienced surgeon, how great that risk is depends to a considerable extent upon the length and complexity of the operation and the age and physical health of the patient. In general, though, complications are rare and usually relatively minor, but may include damage to nerves in the facial muscles (usually temporary), reactions to anaesthetic, post-operative infection, and haematoma (a swelling of clotted or partially clotted blood beneath the skin, which has to be removed by the surgeon). Again, your surgeon should advise you about any risks – and any steps you can take to lessen them – well before the operation, but be sure to offer all the relevant information about yourself, such as whether you smoke, have a history of high blood pressure, allergies, and so on. It is the surgeon's job to evaluate you for the operation, not just factors like your skin and bone structure, but also your general health, but without all the available relevant facts any evaluation may prove flawed. For instance (an extreme example, admittedly), having diabetes may not preclude your having a facelift, but to fail to mention that you suffer from the condition to the operating surgeon could be dangerous.

Having the operation

Once you have decided, with your surgeon's help, upon the type of surgery you will have, you will need to plan when to have the operation and how long you will need to recover. Again, your surgeon will help you do this, and will also instruct you as to what to eat and what to avoid, and any other steps you may need to take; he or she will also tell you where the surgery will be performed, which may be in a hospital, a clinic or similar facility. For very minor procedures, you will probably be treated as an outpatient, but for any operation requiring a general anaesthetic, such as a full facelift, you will generally be hospitalized for at least a day or two. Surgery can take several hours, depending upon how many procedures are being carried out, and for very extensive work a surgeon may decide to operate in two or more sessions. Some cosmetic surgery on the face requires only a sedative and then a local anaesthetic, but most surgeons prefer general anaesthesia for facelifts; in either case, however, you will need to arrange for someone to collect you and to take you home after you are discharged. In some cases, especially with full facelifts, the surgeon may wrap your head in bandages to keep down bruising and swelling. You may also be asked to remain as still as possible for a few days to minimize any swelling. You will need to take care anyway, as there will be stitches in the incision, and the surgeon may have inserted a narrow tube behind the ear to drain away any blood collecting there.

Does it hurt?

The French have a saying, 'Il faut souffrir pour être belle (ou beau)' – 'One must suffer in order to be beautiful.' This should not be taken too literally, however; the use of local or general anaesthesia will ensure that you feel no pain during the operation itself. In general, though, there will be some discomfort afterwards, as muscles and nerves adjust after surgery, but the surgeon will prescribe medication to deal with any pain. Nevertheless, if there is severe or persistent pain you should tell the surgeon at once, and you should also report any sudden change in your condition such as a severe swelling of your face. Any drainage tube will be removed after a day or two, and stitches are usually taken out after five days (but in some cases may be kept in for longer); if your head has been bandaged, the wrappings will probably be removed after anything from one to five days. The skin of your face may feel rather numb, but this is usual and generally disappears within a few weeks, as the skin and muscles settle down. You may be horrified by your appearance at first, though, since your face will almost certainly be bruised, swollen and puffy, but these effects also disappear within a few weeks. There may be some scars from the surgery, too, but these are usually hidden in the hairline or behind the ears or in natural folds of the skin, and will in any case fade with time. Obviously you should be careful of your face and scalp in the days following the operation, but you should be able to take light exercise after a week or so, although you should avoid anything strenuous – again, your surgeon or the nursing staff will advise you about what you may do and what is to be avoided, and for how long. Rest as much as you can, follow advice as to what to eat and drink, and generally take it easy – the reason why some patients feel dismayed or even depressed in the immediate aftermath of their surgery is often because the body is concentrating on healing itself, leaving them easily tired, while the sight of a bruised and swollen face after the operation can be rather dispiriting. As mentioned earlier, though, it seems that most people are delighted with the results of their surgery, and not least with the extra confidence they gain from knowing that they look good.

USEFUL ADDRESSES

The General Medical Council
178 Great Portland Street, London w1w 5JE
Telephone: 08453 573456
Website: **www.gmc-uk.org**
*The GMC is the regulator of the medical profession in
this country, and has 'strong and effective legal powers'
to do so in order to protect patients – it is not the
GMC's job to look after the interests of doctors.*

British Association of Plastic Surgeons
The Royal College of Surgeons
35–43 Lincoln's Inn Fields, London, wc2a 3pe
Telephone: 0207 831 5161
Fax: 0207 831 4041
Website: **www.baps.co.uk**
E-mail: secretariat@baps.co.uk

British Association of Aesthetic Plastic Surgeons
The Royal College of Surgeons
35–43 Lincoln's Inn Fields, London wc2a 3pe
Telephone: advice line: 020 7405 2234
            administration: 020 7430 1840
Fax: 020 7242 4922
Website: **www.baaps.org.uk**
E-mail: info@baaps.org.uk

The Commission for Health Improvement
*This publishes on its website the results of a recent
'national patient-satisfaction survey', conducted by
MORI, which is useful for finding out what other
patients have thought about National Health hospitals
around the country. These results can be found at*
www.chi.gov.uk/eng/surveys/nps.shtml.

The CHI ceased operating in March 2004, and its work has been taken over by the Healthcare Commission (see below); its website still functions as an archive for 'CHI functions and publications', however.

The Healthcare Commission
The successor organization to the CHI (above), the Healthcare Commission 'exists to promote improvement in the quality of healthcare in England and Wales. In England only this includes regulation of the independent healthcare sector.' For cosmetic surgery that is carried out privately in England, it is worth finding out if the hospital or clinic is registered with the Commission, since this will mean that it is regularly inspected to maintain nationally approved standards. The private healthcare sector in Wales is regulated by the Care Standards Inspectorate for Wales. Websites for these two organizations are at **www.healthcarecommission.org.uk** *and* **www.csiw.wales.gov.uk/index.asp**

For information about NHS healthcare in Scotland, contact: **www.show.scot.nhs.uk**

For information about NHS healthcare in Northern Ireland, contact the Department of Health, Social Security and Public Safety at **www.dhsspsni.gov.uk**

The Consulting Room
This is an independent website that provides information about many aspects of cosmetic surgery. To learn more, contact: **www.consultingroom.com**

Dr Foster
An 'independent organization providing information about the quality and availability of health services . . . [It] is now the leading authority on healthcare performance' in both the public and private sectors. For further information, contact: **www.drfoster.co.uk**

Dr Patrick Bowler
Court House Clinics: London, Essex, Sussex
Telephone: 0870 8503456
Website: **www.courthouseclinic.com**

Dr Olivier H. de Frahan (Paris clinic)
15 rue de l'Amiral d'Estaing, 75116 Paris, France
Telephone: 00 33 1 4727 0804
E-mail: **odefrahan@noos.fr**
Website: **www.odefrahan.com**

Dr Olivier H. de Frahan (London office)
Claridge's Hotel, Olympus Suite, Brook Street
London WIA 2JQ
Telephone: 020 7409 6565

Linda Meredith Health and Beauty Clinic
36 Beauchamp Place, Knightsbridge, London SW3 1NU
Telephone: 020 7225 2755
Website: **www.lindameredith.com**

The Joshi Clinic
57 Wimpole Street, London WIG 8YP
Telephone: 020 7487 5456
Website: **www.thejoshiclinic.com**

The Dore Programme
To learn more about the Dore Programme, information
can be found on the official website: **www.ddat.co.uk**